To
Rev. Candace McKibber

With Love

Keep Faith in your heart
Keep Love for people
Keep a cheerful spirit
Keep courage —
          you can make it.

          Sincerely,
Bernyce H. Clausell
          Thank you

No Time To Die

An Autobiography

By
Rev. Dr. Bernyce H. Clausell

Manufactured in the
United States of America
by

**FATHER
&
SON**
PUBLISHING, INC.
4909 North Monroe Street
Tallahassee, Florida 32303-7015
www.fatherson.com
800-741-2712

Introduction

"Lord, you brought me from a mighty long way" is not only a song, but a living testimony of God's mercy and His long range plan for my life. He had it worked out from the beginning - my life, that is. There is no doubt about it.

One day, my daughters and I were traveling down a Georgia highway, when I saw a sign that read, THOMSON. I blurted out, "that sign said, THOMSON; that's where I was born. Stop, turn around, let's go there!" We turned and followed the sign to the place that was a small country village when I was a child.

Indeed, this was a village no longer! Just as I was now a full grown adult, Thomson was now a full grown city; it even had a MARTIN LUTHER KING BOULEVARD. We saw a mailman and asked him where most of the Black people lived. I explained to him that I was born in this town some 80 years earlier and hadn't been here since. The mailman was very cordial as he gave us directions to the black community. He hesitated a minute as if he just thought of something helpful and said, "there's a lady that knows everybody in the community, and I think she will help you. Her name is Mrs. West." He then gave directions to her home.

Responding to our knock on the door was a tall, strikingly beautiful, bronze complexioned lady, with mixed grey hair. She was cautiously cordial at first, but after we told her our story, she relaxed and invited us in. After chatting a while, she told us she was the deceased Pastor's wife of The Springfield Baptist Church located across the street. She volunteered to take us there. My heart leaped when she said the name of the church. I remembered being told that my mother belonged to Springfield church.

As we approached the church I said, "my, what a great monument to honor God." She first took us to the Memory Room. As we entered, it was impossible to miss the elegant picture of Rev. Dr. West that graced the west wall of the room. As we gazed on the picture, he seemed to be smiling directly at you. She told us Dr. West had pastored there about 45 years and was then buried in the church yard. As we toured the church and the grounds, what an awesome feeling it was to stand in the very places where my mother must have stood many times.

Mrs. West told us of a recent trip to New York, so I mentioned that I grew up in New York and I mentioned my friend's name, Anne Bullard. Mrs. West was really shocked and exclaimed, "what a small, small world!" While I was in New York, I was the Women's Day speaker at Ann's church; she's my friend too!" That brought on more conversation.

Now, Mrs. West then told us about a man who just might have known my family. She told us he was quite elderly and crippled, but his mind and memory was clear. His name was Mister Jim. We thanked her profusely and bid her farewell, not knowing we would never meet again. She passed away about a year later.

We found Mr. Jim without any trouble and he was very friendly. He hobbled on one leg, which didn't seem to bother him at all. He invited us in and we began to talk.

"Your Dad's name was Nathan Hall, you say?"

"Yes", we replied.

"My dad was very short, a small man with black wavy hair." Our ears began to grow as Mr. Jim's mind began to flash back and we listened with anticipation.

"Did he have a son called Little Nate,?" he asked. When he asked this, I began to explode with excitement because at that moment I knew he had known my father.

"YES! YES! I exclaimed. Mister Jim went on to say that Little Nate ran off with the circus.

"Yes,! I said, I remember being told that."He went on to point, giving directions to the house where I was born, saying, "it was right across the old ditch."

We hugged Mr. Jim.We were so happy after all these years, to find someone who knew my people! Of course, before we left, we gave Mr. Jim some currency to warm his heart. We thanked him and we thanked God.

We went down the street to find the house where he said we once lived. It was a neat little cottage with a friendly looking porch. It had been well kept over 80 years. No one was home, so we were not able to see inside. We took several photographs with me standing on the porch. From that moment on for the rest of the trip, my whole life flashed before me, chapter by chapter.

Foreword

It is with great honor and humility that I offer these words for such a loving and quality person, the Reverend Bernyce Clausell. Pastor Clausell is a gift from God. Her ministry has blessed thousands with clothes, food, shelter, and most importantly, the Gospel of Jesus Christ. She is a trail blazer, trend setter and transformational leader. Her book entitled "No Time to Die" is a moving and powerful testimony to Pastor Clausell's strength of character, unwavering faith in God, and awesome courage to challenge the status quo.

This book will inspire the reader to never quit; to never give up and to keep pressing toward one's goal. This book is needed in such a time as this; it gives one hope, faith and determination in a God who wants us to finish strong. Pastor Clausell's legacy is that she is a finisher, a giver, an encourager, a teacher, a visionary, and yes, a strong woman with a great faith.

I encourage you to read this book, "No Time to Die" and then, perhaps, the spirit of Reverend Bernyce Clausell will motivate you to hold on until the end.

Reverend Dr. R.B. Holmes, D. Min., Pastor
Bethel Missionary Baptist Church
Tallahassee, Florida

About The Author

Rev. Dr. Bernyce H. Clausell was born in Georgia, reared in New York and ministered in Florida for most of her life. She is affectionately known by a few other names; Tallahassee's Mother Teresa, The State Mother of Prisons, The Reverend Mother, Pastor Emeritus, M'dear, Grand M'dear, Grandma Gar and Honey.

A ten flag birthday salute represents a chronology of her life. The U.S. flag represents her being an American born citizen while the flag of Georgia denotes her birth in Thomson, Georgia in 1916. The flag of New York represents her early rearing by her Aunt Mattie. The Christian Flag represents her surrender to Christ at an early age, and at age 16, professing that she would become a preacher someday. The flag of Florida represents her life after marriage to Rev. James Aaron Clausell. The flag of Florida A&M University denotes her Bachelors and Masters degrees. The Calvary Baptist Church flag represents her being co-founder with her husband in 1958 and succeeding him as pastor in 1977. The flag of Mississippi denotes her famous pilgrimage to Tunica/Sugar Ditch, Mississippi to bring relief to that impoverished region. The flag of Tallahassee Community College represents her honorable recognition in their Black History calendar. The tenth flag, the birthday flag, currently represents 95 years of a precious life.

Rev. Bernyce Clausell is a staple, stalwart, steadfast and consummate community servant; she stands in the gap and trenches, puts herself on the line for mankind, while simultaneously proclaiming God's goodness to humanity. Clausell says of her calling, "God's love and the love of people keep me working and preaching with vigor and vitality. Love will always be my lifeline and my legacy." These are the words of one extraordinary woman, a nonagenarian, who remains very active and as of yet, has *No Time To Die*.

Contents

1

Time To Be Born

To coin a phrase of an old friend Dr. Doris Alston, "That I was born is obvious; what happened afterwards is not." It all started around about 1907 when Nathan Hall fell in love with Eva Hall. Eva was only about fourteen years of age and Nathan was an adult, so they eloped and settled in Thomson Georgia. Ironically Hall was her maiden name and married name too.

My father, Nathan, was a man of very short stature, only about 4 feet tall. He had slick black, wavy hair, boy size feet and could play *honky-tonk* piano. He was the son of Charity Hall who was a full blooded Indian. The only thing I remember about my Grandma Charity is always having to rub her legs. My daddy had a sister named Tilla, and nieces named Julia, Charity and Mamie.

My mother Eva was the daughter of Rebecca Hall. My mother had two brothers and three sisters. Their names were Cleo, Willie, Sallie, Mary, and Mattie. Aunt Mattie would play a significant role in my life later. My mother made a living going from house to house doing laundry.

My parents had ten children. Our Aunt Mary Dunaway was the midwife delivering the first four children. I have no information on child number one and number two. They must have lived a very short life. In July of 1913, child number three was born, my sister Rhelius, who later changed her name to Rhea. Three years later in November of 1916, child number four came. It was me, Rosetta Bernyce.

It was a Jim Crow life back then. Mother was walking from house to house in all kinds of weather doing laundry for the white folks. Daddy was doing odd jobs moving from white boss to white boss. Life was full of insults and injuries for black people in a rural village like Thomson, Ga. "Coloreds" as we were called, were not respected and they were treated like slaves. To escape this kind of life, my family made a decision to move when I was about six months old. They said "enough of Georgia and it's system of dealing with Negroes in a "special-not so good way." They packed up and moved north to Columbus, Ohio where lots of other relatives lived.

In Columbus, I remember my mother always having a large stomach. It seems that my siblings were born in rapid succession, one right after the other. I remember some ladies always coming to the house and taking us off when it was time for a child to be born. Six more children were born in Columbus. Child number five was my brother Willie, child number six was Curtis, child number seven was named Mary, children numbers eight and nine were twins named Charlie and Charlene, and the last child born was a boy named Matthew.

The months and years that followed were filled with heartbreak and sadness.

2

Time To Suffer Losses

A few months after the twins were born, it seems as if the shadow of death took residence in our home. After a few months, death took Charlene suddenly and mysteriously. Sometime after that, my mother became progressively ill. She was diagnosed with Tuberculosis. In those days they called it "the consumption." I guess it was called that because it just took over your body and there was no cure at that time. I also guess that walking from house to house in all kinds of weather had a lot to do with my mom's declining condition. Sometime during the year of 1922, my mother walked through the valley of the shadow of death at the young age of 29. I was only six.

The days between my mother's death and her funeral service were somber, but good days because many people came to the house. Some ladies came and put up beautiful lace curtains at both windows in the living room. They placed my mother's casket right between those two large, long windows. She was all dressed up, just lying there. I did not understand why my mother was sleeping between the windows, but how lovely she looked. I touched her face; it was hard and cold, just like the matching pain in my heart.

The ladies also brought plenty of good food for the entire family. We all had lots to eat. People were sitting around chatting. Some of them were cleaning the house. They kept it clean upstairs and down.

Finally the day of the funeral arrived. It was a Thursday; a perfect day in the month of August. All of us children were dressed up like never before. I don't know where we got those clothes, nevertheless we were proud and pretty. To put more icing on the cake, (so to speak) we rode to the St. John Baptist Church in automobiles! Sadness had disappeared for a spell. We really felt like we were somebody!

At the church there was singing by the choir and speeches by several people. Then the pastor, Rev. J.C. Hairston gave the eulogy. I learned later that was the proper name for a funeral sermon. After the eulogy, the ushers directed the people around to view the body.

Some ladies cried when they looked at my mother. Then, they took my father up to view. He cried and "carried on," meaning he wailed and created quite a scene.

Finally the ushers came to my row and said to me "you may go up now." I shook my head, no. I wasn't going up because I thought I could look at her when I got back home. How foolish I was! They were going to take her to the cemetery after the service, but us children didn't go, they took us all back home. Now I could take my turn seeing her, I thought.

When I got home, she wasn't there. Where was she? What

a painful feeling - my mother was NOT between the windows. My heart was broken. My mother had been snatched from me. These were innocent feelings of a six year old, too young to understand death. Later the ladies explained to us children about the burial at the cemetery.

Life as we knew it was different after that. A stable home with two parents was changed to a single parent and significant others including, Aunties, and a Godmother. These loved ones rallied together to help raise seven children who were disappearing fast. It seemed as if they were dying in rapid succession just like they were born.

Soon after mother died, my one year old brother Matthew was adopted by a family. A few years later we heard that his family had been in a car accident and Matthew along with his adoptive mother were killed. My little sister Mary died soon after that. I don't remember knowing how she died. Then, Charlie, the boy twin, started getting ill. He threw up a lot. I remember him throwing up a lot of beans that we had eaten. He was the only one that threw them up. The next chapter will reveal what happened to Charlie.

My Aunt Mattie decided to move to New York with her family's urging. It was an extra sad day when she left. I remember everyone was gathered around and I spoke words that made everyone sob. I said, "I wish you were coming instead of going." What I said was especially significant because I was a non-talker. I never said much.

Aunt Mattie's moving away hurt bad. It was the same as losing another family member.

Birth Place
Thomson, Georgia

3

Time To Struggle

One day I remember going to school and my hair had not been combed. My teacher said in a mean voice," Why don't you tell your mother to comb your hair?" With a defeated and helpless voice I replied, "I don't have a mother." The teacher never apologized or did anything to help. This is how it was after Aunt Mattie left. Five motherless children struggling to take care of themselves with little help.

A couple of years passed and my Aunt Mattie decided to move the five remaining children to New York to live with her. The five children were Rhea, myself (Bernyce), Willie, Curtis and Charlie. At that time the health department provided services to persons exposed to tuberculosis. So Godmother Hairston, who was our pastor's wife and my mother's closest friend, assisted my aunts in the transition and coordinated services with the New York health department. We packed up and moved; all except my brother Charlie. He was in the hospital and my Aunts were to send for him later. Later never came for Charlie. For some unknown reason, my father stole Charlie out of the hospital, and Charlie soon died.

There we were, four motherless children, living in the middle of Harlem on 7th Ave. in a house with Aunt Mary, Aunt Mattie and her husband Uncle Waters. The health department did their part by providing commodities and medicine for us. What horrible tasting medicine!! Ugh, ugh, ugh, ugh!!

Growing up was a struggle. I remember going to Elementary school in New York; P.S. 119 and P.S. 81; the New York elementary schools had numbers, not names. Let me tell you about a few of my struggles and how they turned out.

When it snowed, people would wear galoshes on top of their shoes to walk through the snow. One snowy day, I wore galoshes and the teacher asked me to remove them. I said, "I can't because I don't have on any shoes underneath." The teacher asked why. I told her, "because it's my brother's day to wear the shoes." After the teacher learned that my brother and I took turns wearing the same pair of shoes, she measured my feet and guess what; the next day she had a brand new pair of shoes for me!

One day I had an incident with a real big girl who was a bully and gang leader. Her name was Daisy Riley. She liked to pick on me. One day she had someone to jump on me and beat me up. After I was beat up, my Uncle Waters came to the school, but the principal blamed me for the incident. I just stood there weeping. A classmate named Elizabeth came up to me and put her arms around me. She asked why I was crying so; "are you hurting?" With a trembling voice I replied "no, I'm not hurting; but nobody in the class likes me." Elizabeth said in a sweet, clear voice, "I love you." That stopped the tears and made me feel like a person.

Now this story has a second part that is almost unbelievable. This incident with Elizabeth happened when I was in the fourth grade. About twenty years later, after I had married and moved to Florida, I was invited to speak in my home church in New York In my message I mentioned the incident that happened to me in the fourth grade. I was talking about love and saying how important it is to let people know that you love them. When church was over, this young woman met me in the aisle. She looked at me and said, "Bernyce I am Elizabeth!" I yelled, "Elizabeth"! We grabbed each other and tears ran down our cheeks. People ran over and were looking. I just said, "This is Elizabeth, the girl in my fourth grade class!"Everybody was touched. They really understood. Believe it! Believe it! It's true.

Looking back on my early teen days, I remember having some sick episodes. One day my nose started bleeding. Classmates told me to tell the teacher. The teacher told me to go back to my seat. The bleeding got worse and I went to the bathroom. It bled more profusely, almost a bucket full it seemed. Then it started clotting and finally stopped bleeding. I went back to class with my dress drenched in blood. The teacher looked as though she felt bad about it, but did nothing to help. It was near time to go home, so I just finished the day and left. It seemed that no one cared. It was a helpless feeling.

As time passed I started having problems with my throat and had to have my tonsils removed. I was in the hospital with eight other kids who had the same operation. All of them went home but me. I stayed another six days. I was slow to heal and felt lonely and helpless. One thing kept me going, I remember that the ice cream was really good!. That's all I could eat.

The onset of puberty was not kind to me. It was downright embarrassing. No one explained to me about female things. About the age of 13, my stomach was hurting pretty bad in school. It was lunch time and we would always go home for lunch and return to school afterwards. The teacher called our names to get our coats to leave for lunch. She called my name, I stood up to get my coat, and the whole class laughed. When I walked to the steps others starting laughing too. Well, wouldn't you know, I had a big red stain on the back of my dress. I didn't know what was happening.

When I got home my Aunt Mattie simply said, "oh yeah, it's about time for that to start." She didn't explain to me what *THAT* was. She just showed me what to do and I changed my dress and put on a plaid skirt so if it happened again, it would not show. I returned to school bewildered and embarrassed. Later that night a lady friend that stayed with us sometime, explained to me what was happening. What a puzzle this all was to me. I was struggling to understand.

My high school years at Julia Richmond High and Wadleigh High were also years of struggle. I began having stomach aches. I was admitted to the hospital with some kind of stomach infection. I ended up staying in the hospital six weeks. Again I was slow to heal. Ever since then, and to this very day, I have a sensitive stomach. I face life almost everyday with a stomach ache.

In my late teens my aunties let me date a little bit and I remember going to the movies with this certain boy once. Upon returning home, he kissed me at the door. At that moment, the door popped open and there stood my Aunt Mary, who saw the kiss. My Aunt exclaimed, "you better watch out, you'll be having a baby soon." Being so naïve, I spent a miserable year wondering when the baby was coming. I didn't even know how babies were made. My Auntie led me to believe that kissing made babies.

Later there was a boy I liked named Ernest Green. My friend named Louvenia stole him from me. I introduced them the day she moved to New York from Virginia. She told me later that they kissed that same night under the church steps and had sex. That was that!

The struggles of growing up brought hurt, disappointment, and sorrow, but some of it had a good ending. There was the time I got a hold of a quarter to go to the hairdresser. That's all a hairdo cost back then because interns and trainers would do your hair. I went there several times before anyone chose to wait on me. I had lots and lots of hair, and it must have looked dry and course. Finally a beautician came and ran her fingers through my hair. She exclaimed to the others, "hey everybody, her hair is very soft!" She joyfully took me in the chair and seemed to enjoy fixing my hair. After that, she would use me as a model to try out new hairdos. Of course, the benefit to me was that all of those hairdos were free of charge.

Growing up in New York

4

Time For Church

Church was a great part of our lives. Aunt Mattie was a gospel singer, so we visited lots of churches. Our church was Walker Memorial Church, with Rev. Saunders serving as Pastor. It was about a mile from the house. We walked every step of the way, every Sunday and days in between. I became very involved in the church. I participated in every auxiliary I could. I loved going to church and was there practically every time the door opened. The church officers must have thought I was smart because they appointed me as a Sunday School teacher when I was 14. They sent me to the Christian Education School that all teachers of the Baptist faith had to attend. I studied hard and some of the students would ask me to write speeches for them. I guess they thought I was smart too.

Sometime later, a peculiar incident happened that taught me a great lesson. I was a member of the Junior Usher Board at the church. We only served once a month. Somehow, members began to drop out of the Usher board. Not me. I JUST LOVED TO USHER. The pastor finally called a meeting to re-organize the board. I was absolutely sure - without a doubt that I would be named President, since I had been extraordinarily faithful. All of the old members came to the meeting. Wonder of wonders; they named Helen Clark as president. She had not ushered in months. You talk about a disappointment.! That was an understatement. I was crushed and hurt. I didn't say a word to anybody about it, so nobody knew how hurt I was. That was a Thursday night. On Sunday afternoon the Baptist Training Union was meeting to elect officers. Of course I attended because I always do. I had no expectations of anything at that meeting. Wonder of wonders, to my great surprise, I was unanimously elected as Director of the Baptist Training Union. Now this was indeed a greater, more visible position than the Usher board. The lesson that I learned and have never forgotten is not to take anything for granted, but to pray about it and wait on the Lord. God will put you where He wants you to be.

The Lord kept blessing me and giving me opportunities for leadership. I was later elected the first director of the youth church. That was a great opportunity with enormous responsibility. Knowledge and skills gained from this experience have followed me through life.

When I was around the age of 16, I was speaking on a program at our church. In the middle of the speech I stopped reading to a crowded church and simply made a statement. In a mild and calm voice I said, "you know I'm going to preach one day." Everyone in the audience applauded and I resumed reading my speech.

5

Time To Make An
Important Decision

The time came to decide which course track to take in high school. There were three course tracks that students had to choose from. One was the Academic course track for those who were going on to college. Of course I saw no hopes of going to college so I didn't even consider that track. The next track offered was the Industrial course track for those who wanted to work in industry. I was not interested in working in a factory so I did not consider that track either. The track I chose was the commercial track. This was for those wanting to go into the business world. This was of interest to me.

I talked to Aunt Mattie about this one day. I told her I wanted to be a secretary. Aunt Mattie made a reply that cut very deeply. She said "girl, you can't be no secretary, you're too black!" That statement was shocking to me and I didn't understand at the time, but later I would.

Later came and I realized she was right. In that day you had to be "high yellow" (light skinned) to get a job like that. Segregation was alive and well, even among the blacks. I read a book called "Under the China Berry Tree." It gave a vivid description of how blacks discriminated against each other, according to the shade of their skin. It was a scary reality. It made me feel very uncomfortable since the shade of my own skin was dark chocolate brown.

In the meantime I took the commercial track courses to prepare myself for secretarial work. That made all the difference. It really paid off as you will see in later chapters.

6

Time To Lose Again

I remember that my Aunt Mattie always had eye trouble. Over the years she had several operations on her eyes after being diagnosed with glaucoma. I learned that the first operation she had was a failure. It was a botched job. It was apparently done by a butcher of a surgeon. Every eye doctor she went to after that always asked, "who messed up your eyes." These doctors did what they could to correct the problem, resulting in about six surgeries. None of the surgeries were successful in restoring her sight. Over the years her sight became progressively worse and I remember leading her around everywhere we went. I remember saying "step down" a lot.

This has become a family tradition. When my children and grandchildren escort me around now, they take pride in saying "step down."

Aunt Mattie's husband, Uncle Waters was a kind and gentle man. I never heard him raise his voice. He helped out a lot taking care of us children. Aunt Mattie depended on him quite a lot. Uncle Waters became ill. I don't really remember him being sick, but I'm told that he asked for me just before he died.

Being without Uncle Waters was very difficult for Aunt Mattie. Besides him being such a kind man, he was a great provider. He had a steady job and Aunt Mattie depended on his paycheck to run the household. It was increasingly difficult for Aunt Mattie to care for us four motherless children without Uncle Waters' income. Things got really hard and she requested assistance from The Children's Society of New York. It was a long time before she got a response from the society, so in the meantime she made a tough decision.

She decided to send the two boys, Willie and Curtis back to Columbus to live. This was devastating to me and a very painful decision for her. The night after they left we went to prayer meeting. I was sitting in the back of the church alone. I saw Aunt Mattie get down on her knees. I listened to her pray that God would take care of my brothers. My heart was broken. It was terribly painful. It's a wonder I didn't burst a vessel or have a heart attack it hurt so bad. I felt as if I would never see my brothers alive again.

It was not long that the news came. My brother Willie had become ill and died. My greatest fear of never seeing him alive again had come to reality. My sister Rhea and I went to Columbus to the funeral. After the funeral, we brought brother Curtis back home with us to New York to live. We were not taking a chance on losing our last brother.

18

My sister Rhea was about three years older than me, and about twenty years smarter. Some time after Willie died, she went off to live on her own. She was working and doing well, but became pregnant. She and the baby's father had made plans to marry, but Aunt Mattie intervened. She turned my sister Rhea over to the Salvation Army who would house her and put her baby up for adoption. And so it was, that three weeks after the baby's birth, sister came home without her baby boy. This changed Rhea a lot. She became estranged. She stayed home a few weeks, but soon left, never to live with us again. She was on her own and quite independent, but she never got over not being able to raise her own baby. She spoke about it often.

Got Work

First Office Job at
the War Department

Second office job

with Dr. Jernigan

and Pauline Myers

7

Time To Make A Living

Around about the year 1936, when I was just turning 20 years of age, Aunt Mattie had found happiness and married again. I called him Uncle Green. He ran a construction office. Guess what! He asked me to be his secretary! This was my very first job. I helped run his office. Those commercial track classes that I decided to take in high school really started paying off. This job made it possible for me to rent an apartment. I found a little place and started living independently.

About five years later, I got a lead on a clerical job with the War Department in Washington, D.C. I got the job! I packed my bags and headed for the capitol city.

My church and pastor gave me a good send off. I was given a letter from my church to take to the Mt. Carmel Bapt. Church in Washington D.C. where Dr. W.H. Jernigan was pastor. I was to join that church when I got there. Having a church family was very important to me. Later I would find out that Dr. Jernigan would not only be my pastor, but would play a major role in furthering my career.

The job at the War Department was all that I had hoped for. My high school courses finally paid off. However, my enthusiasm was thwarted the first day on the job. The cafeteria in the War Department building was not open yet, so a group of us black girls went to a nearby sandwich shop to have lunch. As we were about to sit down to eat, a harsh voice of a woman said "can't you people find somewhere else to eat?" Needless to say, we lost our appetites.

This was mind boggling to me. I couldn't believe this had happened in the Nation's Capitol. I didn't know that Washington D.C. was not integrated. I lost a little patriotism that day.

When the War Department cafeteria finally opened, the whites would not want to sit at the same table with us. If we sat down with them they would move. It made me a fighter as you will see in the next chapter.

8

Time To Fight For Civil Rights

I never dreamed that Washington D.C. would be racist. It caused me to think back on the Civil Rights boycotts I had participated in that had been organized by Adam Clayton Powell in New York City. He rallied the people together to demand that the Woolworth store on 125th street would hire Negroes. So he set up boycotts in which all the Negroes stopped shopping at that particular store. We would stand outside to make sure no Negroes went inside.

I remember a deacon from church walking into Woolworth's during that time and someone pulled him out by the collar. They said, "Man, what are you doing going in this store?" He hastily replied, "I just came to pick up some shaving cream." The response came back, "don't you know us Negroes are supposed to stay out of this store. It was announced in church Sunday." The deacon said that he honestly did not hear about it. He was attending duties in another part of the church when the announcements were made. He apologized and got out of there real fast.

The boycott hurt the store financially and after a time, the store called Dr. Powell to report they had hired some Negroes. When he went to check it out, he didn't see any. After inquiring to the manager, Dr Powell exclaimed, "what!" They don't look like Negroes! "They are as high yellow as I am." You see, Dr. Powell was extremely light-skinned with straight hair. He told the manager, "I don't need them to look like me, I need them to look like Negroes; you need to hire some dark skinned people in here."

Well, on the next visit to Woolworth's, Powell's demands had been met. There were easily recognizable Negroes working the cash registers. The boycott ended successfully.

The incident at my new job in Washington, D.C. rose up the fighter in me again. Me and the other girls joined a group that was started by a group of Quakers. The aim was to integrate all of the Peoples Drug Stores lunch counters. All of the Quakers were white and we would meet together, have prayer and decide where we would go to eat. We were taught not to show any reaction to any violence that may be perpetrated upon us. So, the whites would go sit at the lunch counter and order enough food for two. When the seat next to them was vacant, a black person in the group would sit there and they would share the food. We were cursed at, spit on, our glasses were broken up and thrown away so no one else would use them. Some of us were made to leave before we could finish eating. But we persevered and integration was achieved without violence.

9

Time For A Social Life

While living in Washington, I was introduced to society via a letter that a friend of my Sister wrote to some affluent people. Because of that I became a "member of society." Word got out that I was a movie star from France. I didn't tell them any better. I began to receive invitations for plays, concerts, and other social events.

I was privileged to meet Mary Cardwell Dawson, head of the National Negro Opera Company. I began singing and performing with them; I sang alto. We had fund raisers and sang for charitable events. I sold the first $1000 table for this organization at a charitable event. We sang in prestigious places like New York's Madison Square Garden, Chicago's Soldiers Field, The National Convention in Philadelphia and the Watergate in Washington, D.C.

About this time I became more interested and involved with music. I enrolled in Music courses at Howard University to broaden my knowledge and skills.

I later met and adored the performances of Martha Pryor Anderson. She was a great Orator of her time. She performed with costumes and recited classic poetry. Many years later I invited her to Tallahassee where she performed at Griffin School for a citywide event. She was like our modern day Maya Angelou.

10

Time To Meet My Husband

After a while, the Lord started positioning me to do his work. Remember Dr. Jernigan? He was a very prominent man in religious circles. He was not only a pastor, he was the President of the National Congress of Christian Education and also the Director of the Washington Bureau of Fraternal Council of Negro Churches. Guess what!! He offered me a position as the secretary at the Fraternal Council of Negro Churches. It paid more than I was making at the War Department and it was all about church work which I loved. I started working for Dr. Jernigan sending correspondence to pastors all over the United States pertaining to bills in congress having to do with minorities.

There was an Administrative Assistant in the office named Pauline Myers, who became my dear friend for life. In February of 1943, the Council of Negro Churches sponsored a national meeting at a church in Washington D.C. Pauline Myers and I were the registrars for this event.

This tall, handsome preacher came to the table to register. When he gave me his name I said "oh, Rev. James Aaron Clausell from Florida?" He said, "yes, that's me." I remembered that he had received some mail at the office. I told him where to go to claim his mail and drew a map.

Later that day he happened by our table again. I asked him if he had received his mail. He said "yes and thank you." Then he thought a minute and asked "Have you ladies had lunch yet?" I told him, "no; because they sold out of food in the church dining room." He said, "Well, I'll be happy to take you all to lunch if you tell me where." We told him there were two decent restaurants on "U" Street. He took us to one and we really enjoyed it.

The next night there was a prestigious banquet at the Lucy Slowe Hall. I was on program to read correspondence from the Senators and Congressmen. I glanced Rev. Clausell there and some time after that he told me he saw me when I was reading the letters. He stated that he had to leave that night to be in a baptism the next night in Ft. Lauderdale, Florida.

In June of the same year, Dr. Jernigan asked me to go to Birmingham, Alabama to receive monies he had asked the churches to bring to help support the Negro Council of churches. The next morning after arriving in Birmingham, I exited a building and looked directly across the street. A man was getting out of his car. Somehow, I just watched him unwind out of the car. He finally finished unwinding. You see he was very tall and that's why it took him so long to get out of the car.

At that moment I realized who it was. It was the preacher from Florida. I waved to him and said, "Hello Florida." He asked me "where are you going on this hot day?" I told him I was going to the other building where the meeting was being held. He said, "It's too hot to walk, let me take you there and its quite a distance anyway." So, since I knew him, I went with him. When we finally got to the building I said, "yes it was quite a long way." He just smiled.

Two years later, this preacher from Florida came to Washington to visit me. He said he came a-courting. I didn't have that on my mind, but he was pretty successful in putting it on my mind. He reminded me of when he gave me a ride to the meeting in Birmingham.

"Yes," I said, "I remember that it was quite a long ride. Then he confessed that he had taken me the long way around. The relationship blossomed over a few months. He was quite a gentleman and respected my relationship with my Aunt Mattie. He visited her and told her he wanted to marry me. She gave her consent.

Now of course I wanted to get married in my home church, Walker Memorial, but they were in the process of moving. The new location was an old Jewish synagogue with an auditorium, a recreation center, a swimming pool, a gym and about twenty plus classrooms. Aunt Mattie and Uncle Green had already moved in to live on the top floor because now he was the church sexton. The top floor was 99 steps high, no elevator. Aunt Mattie was blind, but she learned to walk those steps up and down.

It worked out that in September of 1945 we were married in the old Walker Memorial Church. Our wedding was the last service to be held in the old church. It was a small wedding with family and a few friends. There was enough furniture still in there and I was so glad the organ was still there. I loved the sound of that organ when Professor Wiggins played it. That meant everything to me on this special day.

The next day, Sunday, they were able to worship in the new facility. Of course I wasn't there because my new husband and I were on our honeymoon. We traveled to Detroit, Michigan to the National Baptist Convention. In Detroit, we visited a huge garden with many kinds of flowers. We also went over to Winston, Canada which is just across the border. After the convention we returned to New York where he allowed me to stay with my family for a while before moving to Florida. He returned for me in December.

11

Time To Move South

In December Reverend came back for me as he said. We left New York on Christmas Day. We took the train down South to Florida.

An interesting experience happened on the train. Of course everything was segregated at that time. We went to the dining car to eat. I was being escorted by my new husband who was tall, very bright skinned with slick hair, and I was short, very dark skinned with wavy hair. We must have looked like foreigners because the Matre'D asked us, "what nationality are you?" My husband replied, "American Negroes." Needless to say they quickly took us to the colored section.

It was an awfully sad trip for me; I cried all the way from New York to Jacksonville, Florida where we had to change trains. Reverend, as I fondly called him, begged me to stop crying. He said two of his daughters, Catherine and Myrtle would be meeting us in Jacksonville to say hello. They were attending nursing school there. He didn't want them to think he had kidnaped me or something. He was trying to make me laugh, so I finally managed to stop crying.

When we arrived in Jacksonville and exited the train two girls were waiting. He hugged the first girl named Catherine and introduced her to me. He shook hands with the other girl. He gave Catherine a typewriter which he had purchased in New York. After a short chat, it was time to change trains for our final destination which was Pensacola, Florida. He was puzzled about who the other girl was, but he didn't ask. Later we found out that the other girl was actually Myrtle. She was looking very different that day and he was puzzled why she didn't say anything. He had another daughter named Ruth, who was a real puzzle, as revealed in the next chapter.

After being in Pensacola for a few days, Reverend took me "up home" to Monroeville, Alabama on New Year's Day. That's where my husband was born and where the Clausell's originated. It was a very small place. Everybody was related and their last names were either Clausell, Malden or Knight.

It was a gorgeous day, New Year's Day, blue skies overhead and warm weather. Everybody was outside; food and more food was everywhere. Everybody brought food to Sister Chusie's house. This was Reverend's sister who became my great buddy. Reverend's mother Caldonia Clausell was there and took me in as another daughter. I met many Clausell's that day. The one that I stuck with the most on that day was Brother John's wife named Lexana. We became friends for life on that day. Many years later she invited me to be the Woman's Day speaker at the

Beth-el church. They had never had a woman preacher in their pulpit before. Wonder of wonders, they loved my presentation so much that they asked me to come back that night and speak again which I did. Regretfully Lexana became ill and was unable to attend either service. I prayed for her during the morning message.

From all indications, southern hospitality was everything I'd heard it was. Everyone accepted me as family with one hurtful exception.

Our Wedding Day

September,1 1945

12

Time For Stepdaughter Drama

If this was a fairy tale, I would say "once upon a time." But since it isn't, I will say it in plain words. Several months after our marriage, Reverend went to attend the board meeting of the National Baptist Convention in Little Rock, Arkansas. It was my first time being home without him. His daughter Ruth was living with us in the church parsonage. On this particular hot summer night, I returned home after helping to set up for a pre-wedding party to be held at the church the next night. I had just dropped off my niece, Mary McGrady who helped set up. I wasn't in the house a minute before someone burst in the door. It was Ruth and her daughter Ruth Esther. Without any prelude or ado, Ruth bolted in the room where I was, grabbed me and started cursing me.

"You so and so and so and so, what do you think you're doing taking my father's car out all day!" She was furiously beating on me while she was cursing. She clawed at my throat trying to get to my face. I successfully protected my face, as I knew that was her object. She wanted to mark up my face so that people could see the marks. I never touched her, I just protected my face. She beat me good, though. She finally left and took the car.

When she left I started crying profusely. I remembered the words of my Aunt Mattie when I left New York. She said to me, "Bernyce, always keep enough money for your fare home." I looked in my hiding place and got my money. I found a suitcase, packed a few garments and started walking up to Mary McGrady's house. She lived just about a quarter of a mile up Davis Street. I hailed what I thought was a taxi, when a voice yelled out from the car, "who do you think is going to give you a ride, you black son of a b_____!"

Struggling painstakingly up the avenue carrying the suitcase, I cried and cried and cried. Finally I reached Mary's house, knocked on the door. When she opened it, I absolutely fell in the door. "BERNYCE!!!" she screamed. "WHAT'S THE MATTER!"

I blurted out through the tears, "RUTH BEAT ME UP!" She finally got the story out of me and asked me if I wanted to go to the doctor. I told her no because I didn't want the story to get out. Mary put me to bed. I cried more.

As it turned out, I may as well have gone to the doctor because Mary's husband, Frank told us that Ruth was out on the corner of Sixth and Davis yelling out to everyone,"I beat her up! I beat her up!" Frank said people were looking at her as if she were crazy. I really think she was.

It came time for the pre-wedding party that next night. Yes, I went. I had a lovely new dress with a high collar that covered the big gash Ruth made in my throat. I sat there and smiled and talked to all who talked to me. At last we left the party. Mary said to me, "you did great."

The next day Reverend was to return home. Mary took me to the train station in her car. Ruth came to the station in her father's car. We met him at the train and he got in the car with me and Mary. He knew something bad was wrong from the way we looked. He just said, "let's go home and we'll talk."

At home, he and I went in the room and he said, "tell me what's wrong." Of course I told him exactly what happened. He listened and then went in the room with his daughter Ruth. He then called us together and announced to Ruth that she was to move out of the parsonage as soon as possible as she was renting out her own house. She was to also buy a car since she had a good job. He offered to take her where she had to go until she purchased a car. This seemed like a fair decision.

Peculiar enough, after Ruth moved out, her best friend named Odessa, who was also one of Reverend's best members at the church, told Reverend that Ruth's plan was to run me back to New York. Thank God, I didn't run.

But that's not the end of the story. The end happened many years later after we had moved to Tallahassee, Florida. Wonder of wonders; Ruth and her daughter Ruth Esther came to Tallahassee to visit us. Ruth Esther was about to leave Pensacola to live in California. She had just had a new baby girl and wanted Reverend to see the baby before they moved out west. It was a great visit. I made a big delicious dinner for them. After dinner Ruth and Reverend talked and talked; what a great day!

Months later, we invited Ruth to be the Women's Day speaker at Reverend's church in Albany, Georgia; and the next month at Calvary in Tallahassee. So, as the saying goes, "all's well that ends well!"

13

Time For Motherhood

Why is it taking so long? Why can't I get pregnant? I want to be a mother. These are the words that I spoke to God and to my husband over and over again. We decided to see Dr. Aarons, our family doctor. He had us try several things and it still was not happening. This became my everyday plea to God, to grant me motherhood.

PRAISES BE TO GOD!! He answered our prayer. In 1947 we gave birth to a beautiful baby girl whom we named Mary. The whole town of Pensacola was talking about it because this was sort of a miracle baby. Rev. Clausell had produced this baby at the late age of 58; and I was 31, which is a little late to start having babies. In addition to the excitement of middle aged parents giving birth, this baby was so extremely gorgeous, people came from miles around to see her.

The afterglow of having my first baby was dimmed by some unpleasantries. I gave birth at the Catholic hospital, Our Lady of Angels in Pensacola. The staff was extremely strict, very staunch and unfriendly. They would only let you use the bedpan once a day. You had to hold it until that time. Only one nice nurse in the whole place. Thank God for her!

Three years later; guess what!! Another child was on the way. This was the year of 1950. So much tragedy happened this year. Reverend's sister-in-law burned up in a house fire and shortly afterward his mother died and he preached the funeral. In addition to all of the tragedies, I had to return to that same unfriendly hospital to give birth to our second child. I protested to Dr. Aarons and explained to him how badly I was treated the first time. I had not told him about this before. He was appalled to learn about it He told me it would be different this time. He would see to that. You see, Dr. Aarons was the head doctor in charge. Yes, it was quite different. The nursing staff was very nice and attentive.

Dr. Aarons had told us it would be a boy. He was going to be named Aaron Jr. Well, the doctor was wrong and the baby was a girl. We quickly changed the name to Aaronetta. Every body thought we had named the baby after Dr. Aarons, but we named her for my husband Aaron. Aaronetta was the name we came up with to be the female version of the name Aaron. It seems that Aaronetta came out biting her nails. We think this resulted from all the tragedies experienced during the pregnancy. She's been biting them for 60 years!

Many years later, I think I may have had a miscarriage. I had no symptoms of pregnancy, but there were other signs that gave me that notion. Although I wanted to have a baby boy, God had other plans for me.

14

Time To Go To College

While working in my husband's church organizing two choirs, I also had a hankering to further my education. There was no college in Pensacola for blacks. My husband and a friend, Dr. Boyd, realized the need and went to Tallahassee from Pensacola to speak to the Legislature about funding a junior College for black students.

Some time later, behold, a telegram came saying that funds had been allocated for a Fall opening of a school for black students.

I completed the junior college with a desire to go further. My husband and I agreed to let the two girls stay in Monroeville, Alabama with Chusie until I could finish my degree. I entered FAMU in Tallahassee as a Junior in 1954. Graduated Suma Cum Laude in 1956. I was told that my grade point average was so high that it took seven years for another student to match it.

After graduation I felt this strong urge to stay in Tallahassee. I talked it over with Reverend, and to my surprise and great pleasure, he said "Find a house." The wheels started turning and we found a house we liked in a neighborhood named for J.R.E. Lee, a former president of FAMU. We moved onto Joe Louis Street in JRE Lee Park the summer of 1956.

After starting my teaching career, which you will hear about in the next chapter, I decided to enroll in graduate school; it was hard. I went to school on Saturdays and week nights. I would leave my teenage girls home to do chores and sometimes I would take them with me to class. There was lots of library work, typing, reading, and studying, especially for Dr. Boykin's class. I thought I would not pass his class, but THANKS BE TO GOD, I passed his class and all others, graduating with a Masters degree in 1961.

I remember graduation day, which was held at Bragg Stadium in beautiful weather. I was the shortest person in the class and I led the procession of graduates. My gown was so long it dragged on the ground behind me as we processed. My girls tease me about it even now.

Years later I desired to work on a doctorate. This did not come to fruition mainly because my husband objected. He said "there will be only one doctor in this house." He already held a Doctor of Divinity degree; so I guess that was it for me.

15

Time For More Family Funerals

It was during my college days, before moving to Tallahassee, that my Aunties and Uncles started passing through the valley of death to join their sister and my mother, Eva.

The first one I remember to pass on was Aunt Sallie. She was living in Miami where she was suffering from a kidney ailment. I don't remember any details, but I do remember spending time with my Aunt Mattie and Uncle Willie who had come from New York to the funeral. When it was time to leave Miami and return home, great hurt and sadness came over me. I had this feeling that I would not see my Aunt Mattie alive again. I clung to her for dear life, not wanting to let go.

And so it was that a little over a year later, Uncle Green called me and said Aunt Mattie had passed. She had been suffering for some time with an undiagnosed illness. Her funeral was held at my home church, Walker Memorial, in New York City. They still lived on the top floor and Uncle Green was still the church custodian. I remember that my favorite organist, Professor Wiggins played the organ and sang. My, he had a touch that was not ordinary. It was extra-ordinary. On this day I said a final goodbye to my beloved Aunt Mattie.

Sometime later, not even a year, my Sister Rhea called to inform me of Uncle Willie's death. The peculiar story is that Uncle Willie was driving himself in the car and stopped his car on the side of the road, somewhere between New York City and Long Island. An unknown man passed by Uncle Willie's parked car. After the man got down the highway a little piece, he felt a strong nudging to go back and check on the man in the car. When he went back to check, Uncle Willie was dead in the car. It seemed to have been natural causes. I was unable to go to New York to attend the funeral due to illness.

Somewhere around the year 1963, I got word that Uncle Cleo had passed away. That was the end of the line for my mother's family. An entire generation had lived out its time.

While I'm talking about family funerals, let me reflect on the life of my sister Rhea. Rhea was gifted in communications and networking and had a career in journalism. She would make dates for me to preach in New York often. She too was an ordained Minister and started her own church named Good News Baptist Church. Later she became Assistant Pastor at the New Covenant Baptist church of Queens where Dr. and Mrs. Emory Johnson were co-pastors. She stayed with them for five years until she had an inner desire to re-start her own church. She found a building and I went up to help her furnish it off and move in. She had a very good Assistant Pastor, Rev. Isaiah

Holland. He and I worked for days getting the church ready. I stayed and preached the first sermon at the opening of the church in its new building.

Some years later, Calvary from Tallahassee went up to New York; had service with her one Sunday morning and gave a Musical concert that afternoon. The concert was held at Glendale Baptist Church where Rhea's deceased husband was pastor for many years. I distinctly remember when we were leaving New York, we got lost on the freeway. Rev. Holland was in his car sort of leading the way. We lost track of him and mistakenly took the wrong exit. We were praying for divine guidance when we heard a horn continuously blowing. It was Rev. Holland! He swooped back around somehow and found us. To us it was a miracle. To him it was a common happening because he was a long time experienced cab driver in the city. He led us back on the right road to get out of New York. We remember waving bye to the Statue of Liberty as we exited the city.

Around the mid 80's, Rhea became ill and was hospitalized. My daughter Mary and I went to New York to see about her. The doctor told us there were three options: to put her in a Nursing Home in New York, to pay for 24hr nursing care at her home, or to bring her to Florida to take care of her. We chose the latter, packed her two story house, sold it in a week's time and brought her down to Tallahassee. She gradually began to recuperate and regain her independence.

After staying with me for several months, she rented the house right next door to Calvary church, 1107 Joe Louis St. Calvary would eventually purchase this house for it's outreach ministry. Rhea remained very active in Calvary's activities and accompanying me to all of my meetings and affairs. People got used to seeing the two of us together and often asked if we were twins. Eventually her mind started slipping and we moved her back into my home. It was a hard job keeping up with her. She would slip away in the car and once made it all the way back to New York on the train. (That's another long story.)

Eventually Sister suffered a stroke and never recovered. She passed away on Mother's Day, 1993. Her funeral and burial was in Tallahassee. Rev. Holland came down to preach the Eulogy and I presided. I did fine until Rev. Holland began to sing my sister's favorite song, "*I am So Grateful*;" I went to pieces. All of a sudden I realized that's my sister laying down there in that casket!! My assistant, Rev. Donald McBride came to the pulpit to comfort me. I shall never forget his warm and caring embrace in my time of need.

Now I may as well go ahead and share the life of my brother Curtis; he was a homebody. He never went anywhere; never even visited outside of New York City. He did not even come to his sister Rhea's funeral. After being a security guard for many years, he enjoyed playing checkers with the fellows on the block. He was married to Carrie and they had seven children. Two of his children were murdered in their twenties. The first one was a daughter who was killed when some bad men came looking for her boyfriend and they killed her. My sister Rhea officiated over her funeral as I was unable to go. Rhea said they hollered and screamed so much that she lost her patience and walked out. The funeral staff completed the service.

The second murder was one of mistaken identity. Curtis's son went to the store and someone shot him, thinking he was someone else. My daughter Aaronetta and I went to New York and Rhea and I officiated over that funeral. Aaronetta played the organ and sang a song, *Have You Tried Jesus,* which offered great inspiration to the unsaved family members.

Around about the year 2004, brother Curtis took sick and did not recover. His funeral was held on Easter weekend. It was hard finding a flight schedule. The Lord prevailed and my daughter Mary and I went to New York. I officiated and the family started that yelling and screaming again. I went up close to them and explained that reacting that way would not bring Curtis back. I said I would appreciate it if you would allow this service to be completed decently and in order. They cooperated and we got through it. It was sad at the cemetery because it was an unfinished cemetery and there were piles of sand everywhere. There was no grass around the graves, no chairs for the family and almost no dignity to this burial.

After I committed the body, Mary and I headed for the airport. We were even more saddened to learn that Curtis's family had to go into the streets to collect money for which to bury him. We also learned this is the way the "commoners" do in New York. They go out and ask for donations and people give.

Family Funerals

My brother
Curtis Hall

My sister
Rhea Callaway Glenn

16

Time To Teach

In 1956, I got my first taste at teaching when I interned at Riley Elementary School under the leadership of the sixth grade teacher Mrs. Evelyn Brown. Little did we know then that this would become a lifelong friendship. Let me digress to reflect on the fact that we remained friends even after she became ill later in life and moved to Massachusetts to live with her daughter. We were such good friends that upon Evelyn's death in Massachusetts, the daughter arranged for the funeral to be held in Tallahassee at my church so I could officiate over the services. What a treasured friendship.

After internship and graduation, I worked for a summer as the secretary to Dr. Walker at FAMU. When he hired me I told him I would have to leave in September to teach. He asked did

I have a job yet. I replied, "no, but I'm gonna get one." He responded, "my, you sure have faith."

Sure enough, I got one. Wonder of wonders, a distinguished man named Professor Perkins heard about me somehow and contacted me about teaching at Griffin School where he was the principal. He and his wife came to my house to interview me. Have you ever heard of such; the principal coming to you instead of the other way around? He was looking for someone to teach 2nd grade and also to teach music. I fit the bill and was hired.

It was a multi-faceted job. I taught 2nd grade until 1:00 pm, then taught music until 3:00 pm; all in the old white two story building up the hill. Then at 3:00 pm I would go down the hill to work in the office. WOW!! All of my training and experience paid off. Remember the high school commercial track courses, the music classes, and of course my degree in Education? What a plan. It was God's plan! I became not just a teacher, but an extraordinary teacher.

My teaching career covered several grades including 2nd, 5th, 6th, 7th and 8th. I served as chairperson of the Elementary Dept. at Griffin for a number of years. Later I was transferred to Junior High where I taught English and Language Arts. One of the units I taught that I was most proud of was titled "Take A Look At the Best Book." It was a six weeks study of The BIBLE which was and is the best selling book in America. Of course at that time there was a law that there should be no prayer in the schools, but the law said the Bible could be taught as "Good Literature". I had to justify the teaching of the unit and write it up to be approved by the principal. No doctrine was taught, only principles like truth, honesty and courage. Today when I meet some of my former students, they remind me of things I taught them that stayed with them through life. Two of my favorite sayings were "always be a lady" and "always be prepared (the Boy and Girls Scout motto).

I loved teaching grades 2nd, 5th and 6th the most. Some of my students followed me from 5th to 6th grade. I taught them two years in a row. I remember a student named Beverly Pemberton whom I gave a certificate when she finished the 6th grade. It was a perfect attendance certificate. She had not missed a single day of school for six years straight. She married another one of my students named Daryl Lee; and to this day (2011) they are still married, living in Texas and he is a preacher. My star student was Cheryl Seals. She was an all around student, excelling in every area. When she went on to high school, she wrote a paper about me, nominating me as a "STAR" teacher. She has held several prominent positions in life including being on the chamber of commerce and a college professor. She still calls me from time to time.

In the year 1965 the Head Start program was introduced to Tallahassee, Florida. The first class was at my school, Griffin. To my great surprise, I was appointed to be the head teacher in this first ever program. This appointment was made by principal Herman Landers. Boy did I love those sweet children. Some of the children did not even know their own name, they only knew their nicknames. I started teaching them their names. One little girl named Margaret learned to write her name. Several children learned to read kindergarten books, and just about all of them learned to say and recognize the alphabet. In those days teachers made home visits. When I visited some of the homes, the conditions were poor. I began bringing clothes and towels to school to wash the kids that smelled like urine. I provided clean clothes and I also made sure they had snacks. I even had to wash one student's hair. This Head Start experience touched my heart so much that I wrote a booklet entitled, "*Today in Paradise.*"

Sometime after that I moved to the Pineview Elementary school. It was a lovely experience working under Principal Tookes. One of my most remembered experiences there was writing the school song. Little did I know that my future Pastor, Rev. Kevin Johnson, would later be one of the administrators at Pineview and they would still be singing the song I wrote, even to this day, 2011.

The year 1967 was a turbulent year for black students in Tallahassee. It was the year that integration of schools was implemented. They closed down old Lincoln High school and all of the students had to choose a new school. Many of the black teachers were dispersed to other schools. I was moved to BelleVue Middle School. It was a brand new school, just built. It was the first open concept school in the county. There were no walls between the classes. I was taken out of my field of English and had to teach Science for a while. As usual I put myself into my class work, displaying bulletin boards and buying resources to make the lessons interesting. My two daughters will never forget when I bought a baby alligator for our classroom. I bought it while the family was on a trip down state. The alligator got loose in the house before I could get it to the school. It was total chaos in the house. They were desperately afraid to touch it and I was desperately trying to find it, and I did.

We had many other interesting science projects including one that my daughter Aaronetta did as a college project. It was about the solar system. She was a Music Therapy major and composed a song to teach the class about the solar system. She had an experimental group that was taught facts about the solar system using the song, and a control group that was taught the same facts by rote and standard teaching. The results on the final exam showed that the experimental group scored higher by being taught using music.

Of course there were some racial incidents. One white parent put her hand in my face and threatened to hurt me. One or two parents refused to have their child in my class. There were some discipline problems, but all in all everything settled after the first year.

In the early 70's I was privileged to go with an educational tour group to England, Ireland, and Scotland. Our purpose was to study the educational system of those countries. We attended classes and historic places. We were just getting used to integration in the South; but when I went to England I experienced it in a different way. We visited a protestant church one Sunday while there. When I walked in, a little girl turned around and screamed, "mama look, that lady is burned!!" Turns out that the child had never seen a black person before. I must have looked quite strange to her. Another time on the trip a child wanted to touch my face. My skin must have looked like chocolate to them.

I taught at Belle Vue Middle School for about ten years until I had a heart attack. The doctor did not want me to continue working. So there was a very nice retirement dinner held for me at the school; and thus, ended my teaching career.

Since that day, I have met many of my students while out shopping or going places. They always stop me and tell me who they are; and thank me for the principles I instilled in them. My daughters have coordinated a couple of reunions of the students that I have taught through the years. Many of them came and there was a great fellowship. I have seen or heard from about 14 students who have become ministers and pastors since I taught them. I too became a minister and pastor as future chapters shall reveal.

Time to Teach

FAMU Graduation

17

Time To Start A Church

Sometime after moving to Tallahassee, some neighbors asked us about having prayer meeting in our home. Although we had limited space, we consented. Every Monday night Mother Clark, Mother Mosely, her son Freddie, my husband, myself, our two children and a few others gathered to sing and pray. A few months later we ran a Youth Revival. Flyers were sent out over the neighborhood. God's spirit was manifested and six children accepted Christ as their Savior during the revival. We arranged for them to be baptized at Bethel Baptist Church through the courtesy of their pastor Rev. Dr. C.K. Steele. About two weeks later at breakfast, my husband asked, "Honey, what are we going to do with these children that we baptized?" Without hesitating to think I replied, "start a church!". He responded, "I don't need a church." I replied, "Honey, I wasn't thinking about what you needed, I was thinking about what the community needed." (My husband was already pastoring two churches in Georgia). After thinking a minute, he said thoughtfully, "You know you are right, this community does need another Missionary Baptist Church." Therefore it was not just said, it was done. On Sunday, March 2, 1958, Calvary Baptist Church became a living organization and organism. Everyone agreed on the name Calvary and it was voted in unanimously. At that time, we were the only Calvary in Tallahassee.

Rev. began to go out looking for land to purchase. I had my eye on the corner lot at Joe Louis & Arizona. Every time I asked him about it he would say, "but I don't know who owns it." There was no sign or anything on the land, just wild berries, bushes, and some trees. One morning Reverend was taking a walk and ran into Sis. Rosa Walker who ironed for us sometime. The Lord led him to ask her about the land on the corner of Joe Louis & Arizona. Lo and behold, her reply to his question was, "Reverend I don't know who owns it, but I know who controls it." Reverend came home, got in the car and took off. I didn't know where he was going, but when he came back he hurried in the house with a smile on his face. He said, "Honey, I've got the land for the church". I was somewhat cautious and asked, "what land? Where is it?" He said, " right across the street where you've been asking about for weeks, the corner of Joe Louis & Arizona." To say I was happy would be putting it very mildly. I was hilariously ecstatic!!! He had the land and the papers to prove it.! (Hallelujah!!!)

Later in the year the construction began on the church building. We would build a little at a time and continue as we received more money. Rev. and I put our monies together with the little offering that the members gave and paid for everything.

The building was completed in July of 1959. We had the walk in ceremony on the third Sunday in July, 1959, just one year and four months after we were organized. Rev. W.W. Woods and congregation of Tabernacle Missionary Baptist Church marched us into the building. Tabernacle was special to me because I played piano for them while I was in college at FAMU. What a glorious Sunday! That little church on the corner of Joe Louis and Arizona was the smallest church I had ever been a member of, but my love for Calvary is the greatest love of all the other churches.

Now one morning, my husband said, "now listen honey, I don't have time to pastor Calvary. I need to concentrate on my two Georgia churches; so I want you and Deacon Taylor to carry on Calvary and I'll be there when I can." When he could be there was one Sunday night a month. We had good church each Sunday and everyone especially looked forward to that particular Sunday evening when The Rev. Dr. James Aaron Clausell would be preaching.

Each Sunday morning we had another minister to carry on. It was my duty to be sure we had a minister to carry on for each Sunday. Two of the ministers that stuck with us each Sunday was Rev. James McTier and Rev. Dock Roberts. They were great friends.

For twenty years I pastored Calvary without having the title of Pastor. I did all the administrative work, raised the funds, put on the programs and worked with the auxiliaries. I didn't preach because my husband didn't believe in women preachers; BUT he left the church in my charge. He said "do all the work necessary, but don't preach!"

THAT ALL CHANGED as later chapters will reveal.

Time to
Start a Church

Calvary Baptist Church

Organized in 1958

Building dedicated

July, 1959

18

Time To Be A Community Leader

In my life, I have been first in many things. One of them was organizing a children's community choir in Tallahassee. Some time before the church was organized, some children came to me and said they wanted to sing. I played a familiar song, *Jesus Loves Me*, and the children lifted their voices and sang like pros. I grabbed them, hugged them and declared that this would be the beginning of our group. The group was named the JRE Lee Park Gospel Chorus. We performed at schools, hospitals, and churches.

Later the older youth of the community wanted to join. And so it was that 22 juniors and 15 seniors went from place to place representing God and the community.

Sometime later, I took a trip back home to New York. While

there I received a called from an old friend of my sister Rhea. Her name was Lucinda Fox Ward. She was the Vice President of the National Association of University Women. She began to urge me to organize a chapter of NAUW in Tallahassee. (It was then NACW, National Association of College Women). I said, "I've never organized anything like that!" "You can," she reiterated. She was quite persistent and so she won. Coming back to Tallahassee I got in touch with Dr. Lillie Davis, one of my teachers at FAMU. She helped me with it and the Tallahassee branch became a reality in 1957. I served as the first President. I attended my first national meeting in Winston Salem, NC and roomed with Lucinda Fox Ward. NAUW people were very cordial to me and honored me for bringing a new chapter into the organization. The Tallahassee chapter hosted the national convention of NAUW in 1963. Dr. Blanche Gavin was our president then. She was on a trip to Europe during this time and Dr. M. Lucille Williams, vice President did most of the work in putting this convention together.

NAUW was the first black organization to integrate the Duval Hotel uptown in Tallahassee. The organization today is still going strong. We celebrated our 50th anniversary in 2007 and I was the speaker at the luncheon held at the Old Duval hotel which had been renamed the Radisson. NAUW has had many great women as President over the years and they always honor me on Founder's Day.

During these years I also founded the Tallahassee Chapter of Business and Professional Women, The Tallahassee Association of Career Women, The Baptist Minister's Wives Council, and the Tallahassee Association of Christian Women. These organizations wrote their own history, being first in many things. I was not through with community organizing yet. God had more plans for me.

19

Time To Be A Grandmother
And The Other Mother

It was like this: My oldest daughter Mary, had married and now had one child named Clausell Stevens. Clausell was absolutely spoiled by his granddad, my husband. In the meantime, Mary's marriage ended. Lo and behold, sometime after that, she found herself expecting again. Well, you know she came to me with the situation. I went to the Lord and said, "Here I am once more and again. What shall I do in this case?" You see, in those days, it was a shame for a girl to become expectant out of wedlock, so I went to God for guidance. The reply that seemed to be coming from God was "do like some other mothers have done and send her away." That was easy since I had a sister in New York. My sister Rhea had been there most of her life and was known city wide. She worked for the Harlem Red Cross, raising thousands of dollars for them annually. She also was an editor for a local newspaper. Well, good old telephone! "yes, my sister said, send her up here."

That's the story of how Rhea Bernyce was born in New York. Clausell stayed in Tallahassee with us, so I was the grandmother and the other mother. For days Clausell would stand to the door at 5 p.m. waiting for his mother to come home from work. He finally got used to me being the other mother.

When Rhea Bernyce was nine months old, her Godmother Viola, my sister Rhea and Mary all came to Tallahassee to Aaronetta's college graduation. Viola and Sister Rhea returned to New York, but Mary and Little Rhea did not. Mary lived with us at home again, working everyday, and sometimes all night because of shift changes. That means little Rhea was with me a lot. That went on through her elementary, middle and high school years.

As a child little Rhea was quite sickly, fighting spinal meningitis and other medical conditions. But by the time of her teen years, she was in good physical health.

In her teen years, I was constantly upset as I would be called to come to Godby school very frequently because Rhea "was not in school today." Just like some other teens, she had skipped school to meet a boy.

By the grace of God Rhea did graduate from high school. Shortly after that she joined the military. She invited her other mother, me, to come to see her graduate from basic training in Ft. Jackson, South Carolina. We all went. MY! MY! IT WAS COLD. It was in November.

She was then transferred to the base in Ft. Gordon, Georgia. Wouldn't you know, she became an expectant mother there. Don't ask me how, (SMILE).

During the 26 awful hours of hard labor, the baby's heart stopped beating. A frantic emergency call was made to the other mother, me. Now Rhea's birth mother, Mary, was there with her and had arrived a couple of days before labor started, but she is the one who burned the wires up calling me during the birth crisis. On the phone Rhea said, "please go into prayer immediately asking God to touch the baby's body that he might breathe again." Of course I hastily got a prayer line going from Tallahassee to Heaven to God the Father through Jesus Christ.

The nurses and doctors worked hard and fast on the baby. They knew about the Tallahassee prayer line. In about an hour a call came to me.

"Thank God and thank you, the baby started breathing a little while ago." Prayer works! Sincere prayer works! I can testify to that. I have been in seemingly hopeless situations many times; BUT I prayed and God the Father intervened. Things worked out all right. Thank God Aaron survived. Rhea, Mary and little Aaron traveled back to Tallahassee when the baby was ten days old.

Rhea had military leave for a few weeks. When time came to report back, she was told she could not bring the baby with her. To say her heart was broken is putting it too lightly. She cried! She screamed! She moaned! She groaned! I tried to console her, but she wanted her baby to be with her. She also wanted her friends back in the military to see the baby. But no, no, no. Mary had to work all the time, so therefore I became the other mother again in my early 70's. It was fun. Everybody helped me with the little fellow. Aaron is 20 years old at this writing and studying to be a barber. He loves me and is often at the house just to check on me.

Rhea didn't stop at one child; the others at this writing are Ariel, age 17; Allisa, age 14; Mya, age 8. Now, Mary blessed me with two more grandchildren, Bernetta and Tillis. Bernetta blessed me with six great grandchildren; Bernyce, age 22; Mar'rhea, age 16; Jordan, age 14; Justyn, age 12; Brandon, age 9; Jaida age 6. Bernetta's seventh child , Rhian, lived 27 days until his heart failed. Tillis is now in his early 30's. My first grandchild of them all, Clausell ,is now a father of three, Aaron Clausell, age 19, Solomon, age 13 and Elizabeth, age 10.

My daughter Aaronetta has one daughter who is a miracle story. Her name is Earlnetta and she is 28 years old.

So that's the story of how I earned the title of grandmother and the Other Mother. Let me hasten to recognize my other set of grands and great grand children in Texas. The Kinion family are offsprings from Ada Catherine Kinion, my husband's daughter who met us at the train as discussed in chapter 11. There are other offsprings from my husband's first marriage, but the Kinion children have called me Grandma Bernyce from the beginning and have shown me much love down through the years. I must take this time to recognize them and their spouses. Arthur Rudolph/Charlene, now serving in Afganistan; Herbert Alexander/ Brenda, whom I was privileged to perform their wedding ceremony; Linda/ Jimmy, the only Kinion girl; Jake/ Linda; Sharon, Jake's first wife died of cancer, and Aaron/Jan. They too have all blessed me with great grandchildren and great-great grandchildren.

Let me not leave out that three of the Tallahassee great grandchildren have now produced three great-great grandchildren; Aaron has a ten month old girl named Aniya; Bernyce has a seven month old girl named Kennedy ; and Ariel has a seven month old boy named Jayden. I think I'm through being the other mother, but I'll always be a granny, Great granny and of course, some think the Greatest granny.

20

Time To Answer God's Call

The year 1973 brought with it a turn, twist, and turmoil in my life. I felt there was a Divine calling on my life. This calling was to Preach the Gospel. Of course this came as no surprise to me because as written in an earlier chapter, I announced to the church at the age of 16 that I would someday preach. Although I was willing and ready to accept the long awaited call, I had to face opposition from my own husband who did not believe in women preachers. Upon receiving this calling, the first person I went to was our great friend, Rev. Dr. C.K. Steele. As we met and discussed this in his office, he asked me, "have you told

Reverend." I said "not yet." He replied, "well you know you have to." Well, I faced the wind, and told him; of course he was not encouraging. He said "well, I guess you'll have to join the Methodist Church." I had to live with this rejection. It caused me great stress for some time, but I continued to pray for God's guidance. I began to get speaking engagements and I knew I could not get licensed here in Tallahassee. So my sister in New York arranged for me to be licensed by our great friend and mentor Dr. Mdodana Arbouin at her church in Beacon, New York. My daughter, Aaronetta and great friend Versie Young accompanied me on the trip. It was a stormy Sunday that day. This was indicative of the fact that I would have rainy and stormy days ahead, but with God's help I'll make it. Although it was storming outside, it was warm and spirited inside because God was raising up His child to do His work.

I returned home and received a few speaking engagements; but still did not preach at Calvary because of my husband's disapproval.

Sometime later, Rev. Dock Roberts asked me to help with communion at Calvary. I told him I couldn't because I was not ordained. He said at his church, all ministers participate in the communion ceremony. I told him I would help him get the people to move closer to expedite the serving, but that's all I could do.

To my surprise, after church that day, my brother-in-law, Rev. Glenn called from New York. This was my sister Rhea's husband who was pastor of Glendale Baptist Church in New York. He announced to me that he wanted me to come to New York. He was going to ordain me. In astonishment, I asked what date. He said next Sunday. I replied with great query, "how can I do that; I haven't even studied." He said "study on the plane."

Well, I got myself together and my daughter Mary and I traveled to New York the next week and I studied on the plane.

The ordination council was held an hour before the service. Rev. Glenn began asking a lot of biblical questions. I answered them to the best of my ability. The questions kept coming and the answers kept flowing. Soon one of the council members spoke and said, "Rev. Glenn, are you going to ask her the whole book?" Then Rev. Glenn backed down. I had answered every question to their satisfaction. Then guess what! I had to preach the morning sermon. I did it and was officially ordained by the council. I flew home with my certificate in hand.

I returned home with a new vigor. Over the next few years, I continued to carry on Calvary in the way that my husband desired. He began to become increasingly ill. He retired from his two Georgia churches under doctor's orders. Some time after that he retired as pastor of Calvary. A large retirement banquet was held and he was highly honored for his years of pastoring. This left Calvary in a position to call a new Pastor.

The church gathered together one Thursday night. A vote was called and when the night ended, I had been unanimously voted in as the first woman pastor of a Baptist church in North Florida, the Calvary Baptist Church, my love, my all. At last I could be the Pastor not just in deed, but wear the title as well.

After the church voted to confirm me on Thursday night, Reverend came over that Sunday. We were all slumped in our seats, not knowing what he was going to say. I presented him when it was time to preach. He began to speak in a quiet controlled tone of voice. He said, "well I hear you've called a Pastor. You made a good choice. She's as good as anybody else you could get. She knows all about how to run a church." We began to sit up in our seats as we heard his encouraging words. He went on to say that he would be around to do what he could, but he couldn't do much. He says "I'm 88 years old and pretty worn out." He ended by saying, "congratulations to you and may God be With you". He sat down and we stood up, applauding with vigor. GOD HAD CHANGED HIM! WHAT AN AWESOME GOD!!!

On Sunday, November 19, 1978, at 3 p.m, the Installation service was held to make me the official pastor of Calvary Baptist Church. The church was packed with well wishers and some curious people who were there to see history in the making. It was history because I was the first woman to be called to pastor a Baptist church in Northwest Florida. Many of the local pastors did not believe in women preachers, much less women pastors. But thankfully several ministers supported the service including Rev. Dock Roberts, Rev. Dan Speed, Rev. John Ford, and Rev. T.T. Jackson. I have vivid memories of the part of the service that is a tradition in our Baptist Association. It's called the "seating of the pastor." All the ministers surround the new pastor, escort the new pastor to the pulpit chair and seats them three times, one for the Father, one for the Son, and one for the Holy Ghost. The audience stood and roared as history was being made in front of their eyes. This was a special day for more than one reason. It was my 62nd birthday! What an awesome birthday gift from God!!!

21

Time To Bury A Legacy

Calvary continued to develop. Reverend continued to be encouraging to us until his illness took a toll on his life and ours. Around November of 1979, the doctor encouraged us to place Reverend in a nursing home because he needed 24 hour care by nursing professionals. He was indeed a big man, 6ft 3in and close to 300 pounds. He had fallen on the floor once, and we only got him up with the help of four of our neighbors.

Upon the doctor's recommendation and God's guidance, we found wonderful help at the nursing home right near our home, Miracle Hill Nursing Home. He began his stay there which was not quite one month. During that time I had to preach one night in a seminar held at Mt. Pleasant Church. My topic was "The

Angels Are Watching." Two days later my husband joined the angels. The Angels were certainly watching as he made his transition to heaven at 1:30 p.m. on November 30, 1979.

He had planned his own funeral years ahead, so there wasn't much planning to be done. We had three services to honor his passing. The first one was at Calvary Baptist in Tallahassee on Monday night, December 2nd. Rev. C.K. Steele preached who was himself very ill, but sacrificed to preach his dear friends funeral. The Tallahassee ministerial alliance was in charge of the service. The next service was on Wednesday, December 4th at Mt. Olive in Pensacola, Florida where he pastored for more than twenty-five years.

The pastor there, Rev. Bass presided and the eulogy was given by the president of the General Baptist State Convention, Rev. George Weaver of Ft. Lauderdale, Florida. Many fellow clergymen from all over the state attended. Immediately following the Pensacola service, we traveled 80 miles to his home in Monroeville, Alabama for the burial. The eulogy there was given by his long time friend Rev. Lambert from Birmingham, Alabama.

In the following months, I purchased my own grave site next to his and had my tombstone engraved with my picture and birth date on it. I have not yet had time to die, so it still stands awaiting me.

Several years later, my daughters and I attended a funeral of a relative in Monroeville, Alabama. After the interment in the cemetery, we all were standing around visiting grave sites. Our relative was buried very close to where my grave is. So I just stood up by my own grave which is next to my husband's. I was just reflecting and reminiscing over his life and mine when a gentleman approached me. He had a queer look in his eye. He looked at the picture on the tombstone and then he would look up at me. He looked down again and then he looked back up at me. After another double take, he just blurted out; pointing to the picture on my grave; "Is that you? Is that your picture on the grave?"

I smiled and said "yes sir it is."

He remarked, "I've never seen anybody before standing over their own grave!"

It was at that time that my daughters took some pictures of me standing over my own grave. When the pictures were developed, my daughter Aaronetta had a revelation. She exclaimed, "this picture depicts the message of your book!"

She went on to say, "you are standing up over your own grave because you don't have time to get in it!"

Thus, the title and cover of this book came to be.

Legacy

34 years of marriage ended
upon his death on
November, 1979

22

Time To Focus On Pastoring

Until now, my attention was divided between taking care of my husband and taking care of the church. Now the time had come to focus completely on Calvary.

One of the first orders of business as pastor of Calvary was to complete the Fellowship Hall. After many fund raisers, projects, programs, plays, concerts, and help from Thomasville Road Baptist Church of Tallahassee, the work was completed. It was named the Clausell Fellowship Hall. The Thomasville Road Baptist Church was very instrumental in providing supplies to finish the construction. Afterwards they also assisted us in organizing our Sunday School. They provided classroom supplies and training for our Sunday School teachers. They help put up dividers to make classroom space and came on Sunday mornings to provide support. They even donated clothing for our Sunday School teachers to wear. This was a great jumpstart for our Sunday School. We are eternally grateful to Thomasville Road Baptist Church for partnering with us.

We had many unique and outstanding services and programs at Calvary during my pastorate. One was a three night revival. The preachers were myself and Rev. Delwyn Williams. I preached the first night, and Rev. Williams the second night. Both of us preached the third night.

Another interesting program was a Blessing service . Special blessings were given for groups such as all children, all mothers, all fathers, all singles, etc. Several ministers participated including Elder Reginald Peyton, Evangelist Nixon, Rev. Theophilus Jackson and myself.

A service that really drew a crowd was a triple wedding on Valentines Day. Two of the brides wore red and one wore white. It was gorgeous. Each bride marched in while their grooms awaited at the altar. They all said their vows simultaneously. It was an awesome evening of love.

I remember that for the church's 25th anniversary, we had twenty-five services and programs. It took diligence and patience. It was a great silver celebration!!

Sometime after my daughter Mary was ordained, we did a three night revival together. The first night I preached, next night she preached and the third night we tag teamed. Many came out to see this mother-daughter team. Twenty three persons received Christ as their personal Savior that week. What a Hallelujah time!

During my pastorate I licensed and ordained 14 men and women into the ministry. These include Rev. Daryl Hamm (deceased) Rev. Donald Mcbride, pastor of New Brooklyn church of Perry, Florida, Rev. Minnie K. Ford who became Calvary's third pastor, Rev. Eddie Walter Ryals (now deceased), Rev. Angelo Riley, a doctoral student and Assistant Pastor in Chicago, Rev. Cynthia Ryals Malone (now deceased), Rev. Darnell West, an AME pastor, Rev. Deborah Williams, an AME pastor, Rev. Henry White, active in local ministry, Rev. Phillip Figgers (now deceased), Evangelist Carrie Holton, active in local ministry, Rev. Arthur Frison, a prayer counselor and seminary instructor, Rev. Mary Clausell Lewis, my daughter and pastoral assistant at Calvary, and Rev. Kevin Johnson, Calvary's fourth and current pastor.

Calvary became the community church. We were known for our Caring and Sharing projects which provided clothes and food to needy families. We were known in the uttermost parts like Gretna, Havana, Frenchtown and other neighborhoods for having street meetings and outdoor services followed by giving of food and clothing. It was during this time that the community started calling me, "The Black Mother Teresa" and "Talla-hassee's Mother Teresa." I was also known in the prisons as the "Florida Prison Mother" because of the many sons that I witnessed to during our Prison Ministry days. I traveled along with "The Hosto Family," Reverends Dan and Lynn Hosto of Panama City. We traveled Florida, Georgia, Alabama and even went to Tennessee and South Carolina prisons together. They also joined us on some of our street ministries and at the church. When we were with them we were the Hosto Family. When they were with us they were the Clausell Family.

In 1984, Calvary's outreach ministry reached all the way to Mississippi and made history. One Sunday afternoon, my daughter Mary called and began to tell me about a story in the Tallahassee newspaper about the poorest town in the United States, called Tunica Mississippi. I found the article and read it with great interest. It highlighted a community called "Sugar

Ditch." It was given that name because of a ditch that ran through the town with all kinds of waste products running through it. You see, the community had little or no plumbing and the ditch was the dumping ground. The people were very poor living in what looked like shanties.

I was moved to write a letter to the editor, rallying support to help this community of "Sugar Ditch." The response from my letter was overwhelming. Many responded and said they would help. I immediately launched an outreach project that began with collecting clothing, household supplies and money. Volunteers came from all over the city. One family that came was the kickoff for a lifetime friendship; Bill and Fran Lankford. They came diligently daily to help sort and fold clothing and box items. We made contact with some leaders in Tunica through a pastor we met at the National Baptist Convention. He helped make arrangements for our visit to Tunica.

The first trip to Tunica was with a huge truck donated by the Ryder moving company which was driven by Rev. Eddie Walter Ryals and my grandson Clausell Stevens. My car carried my daughter Mary along with myself, my granddaughter Bernetta, and a loving neighbor Ms. Lula Threats. We left Calvary one Wednesday night after a prayer meeting. We arrived in Tunica Thursday morning where a group of people were waiting for us. We started unloading the truck at this place which was a distribution center for the needy. A lady came up to me with a sad face and said, "I need some of that washing powder and they won't let me have it." I came off the truck to talk to the lady in charge. The lady explained that they have guidelines and the people's names had to be on a list to qualify. I hit the ceiling!!

I shouted, "we didn't do all this work to come here for a list. We came to help ALL the people. I demanded that she give the lady the washing powder. I then ordered the goods to be re-loaded back onto the truck and told the people waiting to meet us later at the church. Time came for the church service and it was jam packed with people. I gave them a word from the Lord and told them to meet us at "Sugar Ditch." At that service I met a school teacher who also spoke at the service. Her name was Mrs. Johnson. She was quite intelligent and so I asked her to be my resource person there in Tunica because I needed to make another trip. She gladly accepted.

At Sugar Ditch we gave out everything we had in the truck. I almost lost the coat off my back because someone needed it. Instead my granddaughter took off her coat and gave it away. A little girl picked up a doll that we had discarded because it had one eye. We all had nicknamed it the"One-eyed doll." We thought no one would want it, but the little girl hugged and hugged the doll and took it with her. Mrs. Threats made friends with a little boy and asked him what would he get for Christmas. He said, "nothing." She asked him why did he say that. He said, " because I didn't get anything last year." Mrs. Threats asked him what would he want if he got something. He said a bike. Of course, Mrs. Threats saw to it that he got his bike for Christmas. We came back with an empty truck thanking God for this first trip. We immediately started preparing for the next rip.

Mrs. Johnson, my new resource person in Tunica, sent us a list of needy families with names, ages, sizes and genders. This was very helpful as our committee could begin preparing individual family boxes with their names on it. We publicized our next trip and it was aired on TV. People began to donate money and goods. More volunteers came.

Every time I would say, "we sure need so and so" it would show up. God was all in the plan. The Fellowship Baptist Church of Tallahassee joined in our mission and donated their bus to take volunteers and goods to Tunica. We also had a moving truck donated, so the second trip we had a truck and a bus with 23 people. It was a cold day in February when we arrived. Ice was on the ground, but the people were outside welcoming the bus.

Some of the people took us to their homes. The conditions were deplorable and the price for rent should have been outlawed. There was no running water. Everyone shared a community faucet that was out in the field. No one had an inside toilet. One lady had a toilet sitting on her front porch which the Landlord had never installed. We spent the day making friends, getting addresses and listening to the needs of the people. We unloaded some things at an empty house and told the people to meet us at the service that evening to get more. That evening we gave a worship service complete with music from Calvary's Choir. I preached the word and then we called the names of the families out and presented them with boxes and cash. Once the sermon and presentations were made the people were invited to get what was left which was a lot. It was pandemonium in that place.

People were almost fighting to get the stuff, but God prevailed. Everyone got something and was thankful and happy. After our return to Tallahassee, a couple from Fellowship Baptist Church who accompanied us on the trip, the Leonards, gave a synopsis of the trip to their congregation and an offering was taken amounting in $600.00 to help defray the expenses of the bus.

After these trips, a lot of publicity was given to that town. Politicians began to visit, including Rev. Jesse Jackson and Senator Espy. They began to send in government trailers for the people to live in until improvements could be made to the ditch. Currently, the town is thriving because of the casino industry.

We are planning to make another trip to see the difference that 25 plus years has made.

Because of this mission outreach event, people began to call me "The Black Mother Teresa." They continued to bring clothes and goods to the church so much that we began to have regular give-a-ways, giving birth to "Calvary's Boutique." We stocked clothing for anyone who needed it, for any occasion.

It was about this time the building fund picked up full speed. We began to really feel the need to expand. The "Caring/Sharing" ministry was taking up all the space and we needed more space for Sunday School, fellowship events and worship service. The church was beginning to be filled on Sundays and Calvary was beginning to burst at the seams. The next decade was filled with fund raising and fellowship as the church began to draw up plans for enlargement.

Pastoring

Installation as Pastor

November 19, 1978

Mission Outreach Projects

Frenchtown

Received Honorary Doctorate

November 19 2006

90th Birthday

Gretna

Overseas in Scotland

Sugar Ditch

23

Time To Retire

In 1996, God spoke to me and told me it was time to retire from pastoring, not however from preaching. When God spoke to me I listened and obeyed. I had pastored Calvary for 18 years under my own name, and 20 years under Reverend's name. I was approaching my 80th birthday.

Calvary church out did itself in planning for the retirement. They had various and numerous activities which were held not only at the church, but in the community center and at City Hall. These activities included a Student Reunion of students taught by me in the county schools. There were almost 20 students that attended this event held in the Dade Street Community Center. It was a beautiful program of which several of the students spoke and talked of fond memories of school days. A reception was held in the City Hall lobby in which several commissioners and city officials attended. The Retirement committee informed me that the reception in City Hall was to commemorate my humanitarian and civic work in the community. Dorothy Inman Johnson, at that time a commissioner, was to preside over the reception. A few days before the event, she received news of her mother's unexpected passing. Of course we sent our sympathies as she rushed to be with her family in Alabama. The night of the reception, my daughter Aaronetta presided, after having silent prayer for Dorothy Inman and her family.

On Saturday, Nov. 18th, 1996, an event was held that would make the hair stand up and the chest stick out. A huge parade with floats and all was held in my honor. It started at Griffin School going west on Alabama Street. As you may recall in a previous chapter, Griffin School was where I started my teaching career. This is why the committee chose that location to start the parade. The parade was lead by Rev. Clausell's new found friends, Gary Wadding and a Christian motorcycle gang called "Riding for the Son." A banner was carried in front of the parade made by my adopted son Rev. Augustus Colson. The parade turned left onto Basin street and left again on Arizona street ending at Calvary Church.

There was a great outdoor celebration all day with food vendors, clothing give-away, photographs with Santa, motor-cycle show-off and a live Radio Station with music playing on the grounds. A great time was had by all.

That evening was an elegant banquet held at Bethel AME Church. It was attended by numerous ministers and pastors, including the moderator of First Bethlehem Association, Rev. Edward Gaines. To my surprise, out-of-towners came including family from Georgia and Alabama. A huge display of plaques, newspaper clippings, Who's Who books, photographs, and other memorabilia from my earlier years was displayed along the wall. It was a super elegant evening.

If that wasn't enough, on Sunday, November 19th, I preached my final sermon as Pastor of Calvary at the morning service. The church was packed with well-wishers including another adopted son, Senator Al Lawson, city officials , black people, white people and just plain people. During the conclusion of my message, all of my wonderful control left me and I shed some tears. My daughters told me that everyone cried also.

At the 4 p.m. hour, the final celebration service, the Fellowship M.B. Church of Monticello, Pastor Rev. C.C. Curry was our guest. The Curry's were great friends of the Clausell Family. Rev. Curry rendered a fiery sermon followed by much singing and praising. I will add a sad note here that many years after this day, the Curry's would leave for heaven together, side by side in a house fire. We took the news with a heavy heart, but with fond memories of their friendship.

Back to the retirement service, Calvary's congregation presented me with a retirement gift. I'm holding my breath even now thinking about it fifteen years later. I was told that they had been collecting money since August and that the profit from every event was put in reserve for me. Expenses were kept at a minimum so that there would be more profit. After collecting from all of the events, offerings, ticket sales, vendor profits, and donations from well wishers, Calvary presented me with a $10.000.00 money tree.

Well, this first ever West Florida Baptist pastor from Tallahassee, Florida by way of New York was absolutely speechless. It took me a while to compose myself. I was taken back to know that they loved me so much that they labored for four months, raising that kind of money just to give to me. I was touched beyond explanation. The news was carried through the media, praising the "Little church on the corner of Joe Louis & Arizona"for the great work in honoring their retiring pastor with such esteem and honor. On that day the title of "Pastor Emeritus" was bestowed upon me for life.

A marque stood outside the church, which read, "Happy Retirement Pastor Clausell." It shined brightly every night for a week. That Sunday night I looked at that sign brightening the corner where Calvary stood. I went off to sleep with that visual stuck in my mind. I reflected on the song I used to sing as a little girl, *"Brighten the corner where you are."* That's exactly what I tried to do as pastor of Calvary and that bright marque shining on the corner by the church was a reflection of my works.

24

Time To Pass The Torch

Calvary went along for a while pondering and praying about a new leader. We finally called the Assistant Pastor, Rev. Minnie K. Ford, to be Pastor. Her installation service was one of the most unique ones I have ever witnessed. It was on her birthday, September 14, 1996 and she was looking as beautiful as a doll. As part of the Installation Ceremony a handmade beautiful torch was presented to me since I had been the torch bearer for 18 plus years. The Clausell era as Pastor was ending as I lifted the torch and passed it ceremoniously to the new pastor. My daughters' tears welted in their eyes. It was a frozen moment in time. A legacy was being passed on into hands that were not yet proven to hold it. And so it was that this wonderful Assistant Pastor, who didn't make it so well as Pastor, left on her own will in February,1998.

Calvary went on for another short while without a pastor. I was led by the spirit to approach the church about considering a young man who was already a member of our congregation. His mother and auntie were members also. He had already been licensed to preach by Rev. Wright of Jerusalem Baptist Church. He had joined Calvary a couple of years ago. His name was Minister Kevin Johnson. I explained to the church that he just needed to be ordained and I could provide the training, if they would consider him for Pastor. I further said, "there was no need to read a lot of resumes when we had someone right here in our midst." The church agreed and so did Kevin Johnson. He began his training, passed the ordination examination and was installed as Calvary's 4th pastor on his 25th birthday, August 4, 1998. At this present writing, twelve years later, year 2011, he is still our Pastor! PRAISE YE THE LORD!

25

Time To Escape A Fire

One very quiet Friday afternoon I was spending some time thinking about the organization I had been blessed to start, the Clergywomen's Council United. I had been thinking for some time that we needed a Constitution as a guide for operation. I had sat down to write out a draft of a constitution that the membership could review. I wrote steadily for three hours, using several reference books I had available.

When I finally finished I stood up. My mind told me to put the finished product in the metal files, but I did not obey my intuition; I laid it on top of the file.

Then I turned to my right. OH NO!! IT CANT BE, BUT IT WAS – THE SOFA WAS ON FIRE. I thought I called 911, but our church mother answered.

"Mother Thompson, what are you doing on the phone," I yelled.

"My house is on fire!" (Later I realized that Mother Thompson was #9 on my speed dial; that's how I got her) I hung up and tried to call again, but was unsuccessful. I slammed the phone down and immediately ran out the front door as fast as my legs would carry me. I took a quick glance back and was amazed to see that the flames had actually covered the face of the door and were following me out.

I ran across the street to my neighbor Sister Gosby and spluttered out, call 911! Tell them to come between Preston and Arizona street and not up the hill to the project. While running outside and screaming, I fell in my other neighbor's yard, Brother Ryals. His granddaughter picked me up and took me back to Sister Gosby's and sat me down.

By this time I began to come to my senses. The fireman and police had arrived. I looked at myself. I was all there, my hands, feet, arms everything was in place. I breathed a peculiar thank God as I and the gathering crowd watched my house burn.

Then for some reason I asked about my pocketbook. I told a fireman who had come to check on me, "please look on the floor in the office by the tall files and you'll see a big size lady's handbag." I asked him to bring it to me if it was not burned. In just a short time he came back with the bag. He said the thing that helped him find it right away was the strong smell of White Diamond perfume. Thank God for Elizabeth Taylor.

About that time another fireman brought me a coat that he found in the back room of my house. Right away I said, "Oh no, I can't take that; I was saving the clothes in that room for needy people." The fireman who brought me the pocketbook then said some heartfelt words that I shall never forget. He thanked me for all I've done for others, and urged me to accept the help that would soon be coming to me. Sometime Later I learned the fireman's name was Mr. Flowers, who sadly passed away before I realized who he was. I would like to take this time to thank Mr. Flowers posthumously. Your words still live in my heart.

Both Tallahassee newspapers wrote sympathetic headlines which read, "The Minister who has helped so many now needs help. House Fire!" Sure enough, the help started coming faster than I could count. The day after the fire, my daughter Aaronetta and I were going through my closets for anything that was wearable. The stench of burned clothes and furniture was so strong we had to give up. I was in a predicament, because the next day, which was Sunday, I was scheduled to preach at a friend's church.

I didn't ponder very long. In a very short while, Sister Cassandra Poole and her mother, Sis. Rena Jackson showed up. Guess what. They had gone out shopping for me!! They bought me five lovely church dresses. What A blessing!!

No sooner than they left, another friend, Dr. Carolyn Ryals came by and brought me a gorgeous red/black overcoat. Miracles never cease.

Shortly after that, my daughter's friend, June Sands sent me some designer handbags because she heard my pocketbook had gotten burned. What a mighty God we serve!

I remember Rev. Dr. Holmes coming by, standing in front of the door looking at the devastation. His church was one of the first to give financial help along with the Barrington's church, Metropolitan Cathedral of Praise and Beulah Hill church of Gretna.

Many churches, organizations and individuals helped. God bless the Tallahassee Interdenominational Ministerial Alliance for spearheading a community-wide service after which a bank account was opened to receive enough donations to rebuild my home. I must recognize Mr. Hester who voluntarily parked his truck in my yard and said, "we are going to re-build your house." Thankfully we were able to pay him for his work before he died. Many thanks to the young lady who worked at the Blue Collar restaurant who gave me her own coat because the one I had on was smoky and charred. She said,"I can't have you going around looking like that!"

It would take another book to thank all that deserve it, but even now Lord, I pray that you will hold every person in your hands that reached out to me. May the goodwill they showed towards me be doubled back to them.

I've been through the fire, BUT GOD!!

26

Time To Live The Dream

It was the first Sunday in March, 2008, a sunny clear day, parking lot full, capacity seating. The occasion was the 50th anniversary of my beloved Calvary Baptist Church. Smiles were on every face and excitement was in the air. The announcement was made, the music started and the procession began. You see this was not just an anniversary celebration, it was the grand opening of the NEW Calvary Baptist Church, located at 1915 Dale St. It was the ultimate golden anniversary gift. God had given Calvary a new home. Yes, we had moved from our beloved 1101 Joe Louis Street to the church that God built for Calvary.

It's amazing how it all unfolded. The church had been raising money for the building fund for 25 or more years. It was our dream to enlarge the Joe Louis St. church. The news came from the city somewhere in the year of 2006, that we would not be approved to build there on our current lot. There was not enough land to do what we needed done. Also, it would cost at least $350.000.00 to do all that the city requested. I asked Pastor Johnson if we could start looking around for a building that's already in use; he gave the go ahead.

It all started when my daughter Aaronetta spoke to a realtor friend. She got on it right away and had Aaronetta meet her at a certain address. She had never heard of this street before, but it was 1915 Dale St. It was a vacant church building with pews and furniture already in it; equipped with baptismal pool, classrooms, office space, and an annex which was once used as a daycare. She came home and told me about it. I called the pastor and we met at the church the next morning. We put in an application to purchase, and it was not approved. We sort of gave up the search.

About a year passed and I got the unction to seek for a church building again. Soon one morning I called a well known real estate agency. I told them that we were interested in a church building that was already up. He said, "Rev. Clausell we have two; do you want to see them?"

"Yes!" I replied. We agreed to meet at the first church the next morning at 10 a.m.

When we arrived there, I was quite surprised. I told the agent, "we looked at this place over a year ago. I told him how we had applied for the loan without success. The agent said, "you might can get it now." I asked, "why, why now?" He replied, "because it's back on the market." After touring through the building again, we thanked the agent and told him that we would call him later. We never did see the other building.

A peculiar feeling came over me as we left. I told Aaronetta that I wanted to see Mr. Lambert. Now, Mr. Lambert was the contractor that was going to rebuild Calvary on Joe Louis street. Aaronetta did not hesitate. She said, "okay, I'll take you now."

Arriving at Mr. Lambert's office, his wife/receptionist welcomed us warmly. Mr. Lambert heard our voices and came out to meet us. "Why good morning, Rev. Clausell and daughter; how are you ladies this fine day?"

We replied, fine thank you." I cut right in and blurted out that we saw a building this morning that we liked. I told him it was across town on Dale Street. "Dale Street," he replied. He then broke in excitedly and informed us that he knows the man that holds the mortgage on that building; he asked if I wanted his telephone number. Of course we wanted the number!!! We were just standing there in awe. It's a miracle how God leads those who are willing to follow!

As we were coming out of our near-faint condition, (smile) we heard him say, "here's the name and number;" you call him when you get home. He added, "by the way, I know the banker too. All three of us have a prayer breakfast every Monday morning." By this time we were ecstatic and almost speechless. That confirmed why I had that peculiar feeling that I needed to see Mr. Lambert. We thanked him profusely as we left the office and thanked God all the way home for his wondrous works.

The next morning the phone rang. The voice on the other end said, "this is Dan Winchester, I heard you want to talk to me; I own the church on Dale Street. I was awe-struck all over again. I never expected that the owner would be calling me, of course it usually works the other way around. We talked for a while and he said he had other offers on the building, but he would hold it until we could work with the bank.

Pastor invited Mr. Don May of Farmer's & Merchants Bank to come and address the congregation about the terms of a contract. In the business meeting that followed, the church voted to go forth with the application process.

Meanwhile, Aaronetta and I went on vacation to visit the Lankford's in Wisconsin. While there all I could think about was the church. I wondered, "will we get approved?"

I called Mr. May from Wisconsin to inquire about the status of the application. I was holding my breath when he said, "looks like we can do it." We all rejoiced over the great news. We shouted out praises to God right in the Lankford's house. They backed up their shout with a monthly pledge of $50.00 toward our mortgage for as long as it takes. To this day, three years later, they have not missed sending their pledge.

The rest is history; a dream became a reality on March 2, 2008. On that beautiful God-given day, Calvary's golden anniversary, Pastor Johnson presented me with a plaque with actual doors that opened like a church. Inside the doors is a picture of the new church with the words, "To Calvary's Dreamer. Thanks for leading us into the Promised Land."

27

Time To Celebrate

Our Pastor, Rev. Johnson, continues to honor me and recognize my birthday every year. During my birthday month, each November, he designates the birthday weekend as Homecoming Weekend at Calvary. We invite former members to be with us, participate on the program and just fellowship. Each year it's like a reunion seeing people that I baptized as children, all grown up. Some of them are preachers now and have been invited back to preach on programs at Calvary.

The 88th birthday celebration was a whopping big one. It was a banquet at the Ramada Inn. It seemed like there were about two hundred people there. Our out-of-town guests were Bill and Fran Lankford of Naples, Florida, the couple we met during the Mississippi outreach project. A limousine took us to the banquet and we were escorted to our places by men in uniform. My daughter Aaronetta was on the microphone as she narrated a ten flag salute to my life. This salute has been included in my biography. The banquet speaker was Dr. William Law, President of Tallahassee Community College, who sacrificed the famous Florida State/Florida football game to be with us. This was truly a night to remember.

The 90th birthday was unmatched. It included a Saturday night reception program at Bethel AME banquet hall which was on open microphone program. Out of town relatives included the Hawes-Jones family of New York, Herbert and Brenda Kinion of Texas, The McCormick Family of Milllidgeville, Georgia, and Elder Trenton Lambright of South Carolina. Commissioner Cliff Thaell and his wife presided over the event. My family presented a DVD of a synopsis of my life that everyone was touched by.

The next day, Sunday, the celebration was continued with Rev. Alonzo Ford preaching at the 11am service at Calvary. Alonzo Ford grew up in Calvary and now has his own Ministry in Mississippi. At 3 p.m, there was another service and many surprises. The first surprise was to see my spiritual son Rev. Dr. Angelo Riley. He flew in from Chicago and was the speaker for the occasion. My family kept this a secret and boy what a sweet surprise it was. The greatest surprise and honor was presented by my pastor, Rev. Kevin Johnson. He knew the story of how I never fulfilled by desire to earn a doctorate. I don't know how he did it, but he presented me with an honorary doctorate degree from Kings Cross Victory Bible College, along with a doctoral robe. I was almost paralyzed with surprise and humility. For many minutes I could not speak for catching my breath and wiping my tears. I don't believe there was a dry eye in the house. Everyone was touched. This was the birthday of birthdays. Thank you again Pastor Johnson!!!

Every year, Pastor Johnson and my daughters continue to honor me to the highest. The 93rd birthday celebration featured Senator Al Lawson as the speaker. One of the highest honors I have ever received was presented by Pastor Rosalyn Thompkins. It was the 2008 Presidential Volunteer Service Award, on behalf of President Obama's National Council of Service and Civic Participation. This award came all the way from the White House into my house. What an overwhelming honor! The 94th birthday featured Pastor Rosalyn Thompkins as speaker. Among the special guests was a cousin I had never met, Rev. Russell Clausell and his wife of Dothan, Alabama.

Music for the celebrations has always been special including, the Maranatha, 7th Day Adventist Choir, Cassandra & Anthony Poole, Greater Mt. Pleasant Choir, Fred Lee, and the most talented Tallahassee Girl's choir of choice with Dr. Rose Hill, Director.

I don't know how many more celebrations there will be, but during this 95 year journey I have walked the walk, talked the talk, prayed prayers, and sang songs to God's glory. As the scripture says in Matthew 25: 36-37, I have given meat to the hungry, water to the thirsty, took in strangers, clothed the naked, visited the sick, preached to the imprisoned, and given to the poor. Often I get weak, but everyday I raise my aching arms in praise for a new day, my limp legs cut a step when I think of His goodness, and my voice is raised in victory because death has been defeated.

It's been a great ride from Thomson, Georgia. to where I am now, and God is not through with me yet. He keeps giving me assignments and I keep carrying them out. I know that someday I'm going to be with Jesus and live in the heavenly home He has prepared for me, but right now I keep so busy working for my Jesus, I've got "NO TIME TO DIE."

It is best said in the words of the old Negro Spiritual, *Ain't Got Time To Die.*

>Lord, I keep so busy working for my Jesus
>Keep so busy working for my Jesus
>Keep so busy working for my Jesus
>Ain't got time to die.
>
>Lord I keep so busy serving my Jesus
>Keep so busy serving my Jesus
>Keep so busy serving my Jesus
>Ain't got time to die.
>
>Lord I keep so busy praising my Jesus
>Keep so busy praising my Jesus
>Keep so busy praising my Jesus
>Ain't got time to die
>
>Cause it takes all of my time to praise my Jesus
>All of my time to praise my Lord
>If I don't praise Him the rocks are gonna cry out
>Glory and Honor! Glory and Honor!
>AIN'T GOT TIME TO DIE!

28

Time For Others To Reflect

One of my mottos in life has been like the song, "if I can help somebody as I pass along, then my living will not be in vain." Well, that saying works in the reverse as well. Many somebodies have helped me and their lives will not be in vain. My life has been sweetened with kind words, accolades and awards from people and organizations that honored me and my work . Many plaques line the walls of my home and many sweet words and tokens of love adorn the shelves and tables.

Many have watched and witnessed my life and my work and have told me that I inspired them to preach, teach and write. The following pages are reflections and testimonies from persons with whom I am proud to have shared this life.

From The First Born Child, Rev. Mary Clausell Lewis

When we talk about angels, you would be talking about my mother the Rev. Dr. Bernyce Hall Clausell. She is the reason I am who I am today. She taught us children the purpose of life and to live the ways of the bible. She taught us the value of a dollar and how to spend it. She also taught us how to love others and get your blessings.

When we talk about angels, let me give you a couple of examples of what I am talking about. I remember when I had my first child; it was a very difficult time for me especially because of my broken marriage. After I gave birth, my mother came to the window to see this eight-pound baby boy that was her first grandchild. She fainted on the floor! I guess the thought of her daughter going through all that pain and labor overwhelmed her. She recovered and helped me raise him with her wisdom, over 40 years now.

I remember the time I was scheduled to have back surgery. M'dear was not feeling well so I called her the day before the surgery. She told me she would not be able to come. I told her I understood and I knew she would be praying for me. She asked me what time was the surgery and I told her 6 a.m. She said, "don't be scared because the Lord is with you and so am I." Well, I was satisfied with that, even though I really wanted my mother there. I went on to sleep and put my trust in God like she had taught me to do.

The next morning when they were preparing to roll me into surgery, who came walking in, my mother, my angel! I said,

"Mother, I thought you were not feeling well." She replied, "it did not matter how I felt, I knew my daughter needed me, so here I am." Well that was the icing on the cake for me. After a few days in the hospital, I was transferred to Rehabilitation. It was so disappointing because I had to be there on Mother's Day. What a bummer, but I took it in stride. On Mother's Day afternoon, I was sitting in the day room. I looked up and who did I see; my own dear mother. She looked just like an angel wearing a beautiful white hat with silver streaks. It looked like she had a halo on her head. I said "there's my angel." It really touched my heart for her to be there because she herself should have been in bed. It was like a message from the Lord telling me that everything is okay and my mother was the sign. One of my mother's favorite sayings is, "it's GOOD to be seen." When I saw my mother that day, I knew everything was GOOD and VERY GOOD.

Good things come in three's, like the Trinity. The third memory I want to share is when my husband W.C. Prather was buried. I was already scheduled to give my first sermon the day after his funeral. When this sermon was scheduled, he was alive and well. No one would have ever guessed that I would be burying my husband the same weekend. We decided not to re-schedule. I prayed for strength to get through it. When it was time for me to walk toward the pulpit to deliver my sermon, my mother came, stood by me, and asked if I wanted her to pray. All I could do was nod my head yes. She prayed a prayer of strength that took me through that sermon from the first word to the last one. Again, there she was, my angel, appearing in all her glory, to spread her wings over me and lift me up.

Even though she had to clip my wings a few times through life, (as mothers do) she always covered me with hers and continually set me on my flight. Because of her wings, I can fly!

From The Second Born Child, Aaronetta Clausell Frison

A hero, superwoman, role model, mentor, are all labels that describe my mother-dear. She didn't just teach us how to live life in the right way, she showed us. From early years she exposed us to the things that really counted in life. Having been around M'dear for 61 years now, I have a pretty good picture of what a meaningful and purposeful life should be like. I'm still striving to get there. Being a senior citizen now, I sometimes look back on the impressionable years of my life and reflect on events that helped mold me.

My parents taught me to read at an early age and my comprehension was good. As a matter of fact I remember being told that I made the highest score on the first grade Achievement Test. I attribute that to my parents. Because of my early ability to read and comprehend, I remember reading a message on a wall plaque at my parent's home around the age of six. The plaque read, "Only one life, will soon be passed. Only what's done for Christ will last." That saying has guided me and has had a lasting impact on my life.

At a young age, I began to wonder, what can I do for Christ. I didn't have to guess. My M'dear was already doing it. All I had to do was model her. So, there my life went, following her around to church meetings, school, choir rehearsals and programs. I got top notch hands on experience of how to be a Christian, an educator, an organizer, a wife and mother.

She worked overtime as a teacher. Every holiday we were in her classroom helping fix bulletin boards and cleaning up. Can't forget the times I wanted something out of the store but instead she bought stuff for the students in her classroom. When we had church in our house, she coached me how to be a Sunday School teacher. When she saw my interest in ballet, because our next door neighbor was a dance instructor, she let me compose a dance with her students. We performed the dance, "Waltz of the Flowers" at a PTA assembly. We had costumes and all. She started us with Music lessons at an early age and bought me a cornet to play in the school band. My band teacher said I would have "strong kisses," because few girls played trumpet. (at that time).

When I was in about 8th grade, a young neighbor became pregnant. We were the same age. One day while M'dear was braiding my hair, she talked to me about the "birds and bees." She said, "it is a sin to let a boy touch you before time." She made it plain that the right time was upon marriage. I remember asking, "wouldn't God forgive us if we ask Him and don't do it again?" She replied, "yes, He's a forgiving God, but the damage is already done after the first time." I followed up with another question, "what are the damages?" When she finished telling me about pre-marital pregnancy, disease, doctor's visits, pelvic exams, pap smears and infections, I was too afraid to even look at a boy.

Through all the stages of my life, M'dear has been there to teach me, comfort me, and encourage me. As I look back on her life's journey, how she sacrificed for us, how she was always helping somebody and how she was "always a lady," I wish nothing but to give back to her the good life she gave to me.

By the way, I still have that wall plaque from childhood hanging in my house.

From The Adopted Son, Augustus Colson

Mother Bernyce H. Clausell, an aging but mighty warrior adopted and volunteered to council and defend a novice soldier son through the hard times of a decision to go to journalistic war. His almost impossible task was to be performed against all odds-without complaining. My first strict instructions demanded that I never bash the church, follow the dream that God gave and ignore everyone and everything else.

Once I made it through the initial instructions in persistence, determination and endurance, Mother Clausell fought many of the other unknown physical battles for me. More than all that she means to me, she calls me Son.

Augustus Colson

Tribute to Pastor Bernyce Clausell

I am eternally grateful for Pastor Bernyce Clausell for the support that she has rendered to me during my entry into the ministry. As a deacon of Calvary Missionary Baptist Church in 1978, it was she who saw the calling of God on my life as a preacher. I knew it was upon me but I did not think anyone else saw it. Was I mistaken? Yes!

It was a scene that I will not forget. After evening worship service, Pastor Clausell called me to her home. She got straight to the point. I was totally unprepared. Standing over my seated six-foot frame, she said God has called you to preach. I could say nothing but hang my head. I was caught! She talked and then she prayed. I have been formally preaching ever since.

I say formally because I have been preaching all my life. Even as a child at home, I would imitate my pastor, H.W. Wilburn, of New Salem M.B. Church in Tampa, Florida. I would conduct funerals of dead birds, cats, frogs, and doll babies. Preaching was and is in my blood.

I have completed my silver anniversary as Pastor of New Brooklyn M.B. Church, Perry, Florida in June, 2011. Glory to God for all that He has done.

Written in love,
Donald McBride

Rosalind Y. Tompkins, Pastor
Turning Point International Church of Tallahassee

I first noticed Rev. Clausell when I saw her at various community and church events wearing her clergy collar oftentimes in the midst of a sea of male clergy. I admired this phenomenal Woman of God from afar, because of her quiet dignity and strength as she touched the untouchable and loved the unlovable. Much to my pleasant delight and surprise, I was summoned to Rev. Clausell's church for a special service where they were honoring those they admired in the community. As a founder and director of Mothers In Crisis, I had spent several years helping to free women from drugs and alcohol as I nursed and protected my own recovery. I had no idea this powerful woman of Grace and Purpose even knew my name. So when I was told that Rev. Bernyce Clausell had picked me out as a role model, I was humbled to the core of my being. With tears in my eyes I went to the service and received the honor, but most importantly, I gave honor to God for allowing us to come together. We have been friends from that day to this, as she enriches and adds value to my life and the lives of generations to come.

Dr. Elmira P. Davis, Pastor
New Destiny Church of Christ Written In Heaven
of Tallahassee

Rev. Bernyce Clausell is an articulate, quick thinking, straight shooting, scripture quoting leader who is my mentor, predecessor, and fellow laborer in the Gospel. As she moved from the front line to the sidelines, it was with humility and honor that I accepted the torch to succeed her as president of the Clergywomen's Council United, Inc. Even though she is barely five feet tall and 100 pounds soaking wet, I realized and appreciated that I was indeed standing before a spiritual GIANT. Rev. Clausell is still a welcomed and inspirational presence at all our meetings and shares much wisdom with those present. We appreciate and treasure this precious "jewel" that God placed in our midst. We never miss an opportunity to honor and validate this mother, civil rights pioneer, grandmother, pastor emerita, retired educator and now author.

If You Got To Be Small
By Rev. Willie Ryals – Son in the Ministry

If you're traveling and need directions,
If you need friends, make good selections.
If you meet a giant so tall;
become as a baby, you got to be small.
If the street you're traveling comes to a dead end;
If the world around you is full of sin,
If you're climbing a ladder about to fall,
become as a baby, you got to be small.
Friends come and friends go;
people laugh because they don't know,
People talk because favors aren't fair,
just look to the One, the One who cares.
If you're afraid and the way seems dark,
If you need faith and a brand new start;
Just raise your hands to the All in All,
become as a baby, you got to be small.

No Time To Die
By Rev. Willie Ryals – Son in the Ministry

Let there be no questions about tomorrow
There's no time for tears or sorrow.
As I travel in God's love I bask,
I still find just another task.
So let my life show the way
To every child whose gone astray
Children this is no time to cry
For I know its NO TIME TO DIE!

My fifth and sixth grade teacher
By Cheryl Seals Mobley Gonzalez

I recall having very strong matrons as teachers at dear ol' Griffin elementary School in Tallahassee. Mrs. Bernyce Hall Clausell taught me not once, but twice in both fifth and sixth grades. She led the way in things that mattered like life, liberty, the pursuit of happiness, and loving your neighbor as yourself. I had no idea that the songs she taught us and the strong drive to compel us to succeed in the face of adversity would come into play many, many times and years later. The songs were not soulful, fleshy songs heard on record albums. They were soulful Christian and patriotic songs like:

"If I have wounded any souls today, if I have caused one foot to go astray, If I have walked in my own willful way, Dear Lord, forgive."

Another song was "Satisfied with Jesus" and we learned to love our country through the song "This Land is Your Land."

Mrs. Clausell influenced a lot of her students to go to church and would pick them up in her car. She used her Christian influence to guide our everyday life. I'll never forget the complaint she made about the brand new majorette uniforms that we modeled in faculty meeting one day. She said right out in the meeting, "they are pretty, but skimpy and need a skirt". I also remember when she was my Girl Scout leader, she again used her Christian influence to create a Bible badge. We were probably the only troop in the whole nation that wore a Bible Badge on their sashes.

Her petite stature has not hindered her from being a giant in the community. She has outlived many of her students and I am blessed and thankful to still be here to write this testimony.

109

I Honor You
Herbert Alexander, grandson

I tell you the truth, there are not many words I can say to describe the kind of impact and influence Rev. Dr. Bernyce Clausell, my grandmother, has had on society and the world. She has been a spiritual leader through her long and blessed life. I can imagine the Lord saying to her on that glorious day with the angels rejoicing, "Well done my good and faith servant, for you have been faithful with a little and I will now make you ruler over much in heaven!

I confess, Rev. James A. Clausell, my grandfather and my grandmother have had the greatest spiritual influence on my life than any other spiritual leader has ever had in my life since Childhood. You see, I was a bad boy in my childhood and was voted by many most "unlikely" to succeed. However, my grandfather would always try to lead me on the path of righteousness and when my grandmother came around, it was like the demons had to go and it was hard to be bad when she was present. My grandmother had a firm hand with me which is what I needed as a child.

Well, as a minister today, I think back on my life and thank God for allowing her to be a blessing to me when I needed it. I think of her as a Proverbs 31 woman. Her life has been about providing shelter for the poor, spiritual counseling for the weak, winning souls of sinners, preaching gospel to the saints and bringing together what no man should put asunder. She had a chance to meet my fiancé, Dr. Brenda Kinion, who is now my wonderful wife, when we visited her on her 90th birthday. The two of them hit it off so well that Brenda wanted Grandmother to perform the wedding ceremony at her church in Tallahassee. We were truly honored to have grandmother marry us at her legacy church, Calvary Baptist Church on 07/07/2007. I thank my family and friends for traveling from Texas and other parts to celebrate this special time in our lives and to see grandmother in her prime. God keeps taking her from Glory to Glory and He is not through with her yet. Heaven can wait, for there is still too much work to be done for the Kingdom and it is *No Time To Die.*

Appendix A

The following pages lists out awards, plaques, proclamations, newspaper, magazine articles, and other recognitions of honor bestowed upon this writer. Some may be omitted due to being destroyed in the house fire, or due to human error. My apologies are extended for any omissions, but please know that the memories remain forever written in my heart.

December. 1965 – *Tallahassee Democrat* – "Couple Married Twenty Years Weds Again"
December, 1976 – *Tallahassee Democrat* – "Drifters, Inc. honors Beautiful Activists"
January, 1977 – Certificate of Ministerial Ordination presented by Pastor Robert Glenn, Glendale Baptist Church, New York.
September, 1978 – *Tallahassee Democrat* – She is Spreading the Word Of God
    ? 1983 – *Tallahassee Democrat* – "Teacher Questions Educational Priorities"
October, 1984 – *Tallahassee Democrat* – "Commission to Fill Vacancy on City Board"

August, 1985 – *Tallahassee Democrat* – "People of Sugar Ditch Need our Help"

October, 1985 – *Tallahassee Democrat* – "Tallahassee to Tunica"

November, 1985 –*Tallahassee Democrat* - "Tallahassee to Tunica: Mission Accomplished"

December, 1985 – *Tallahassee Democrat* – "Sugar Ditch will Make You Thankful

January, 1986 – NAACP – Martin Luther King Jr. Community Service Award

March, 1986 – National Association of University Women Appreciation Award

May, 1986 – First Bethlehem Association, Pastor of the Year Award

November, 1986 – *Gadsden County Times* – "Poverty in Gretna Moved Her To Give"

November, 1986 – *Tallahassee Democrat* – "Teacher Who Became Preacher Is Honored"

?   1989 – Writer V.S. Naipaul devotes a passage in his book to Rev. Clausell, book title, *A Turn In The South*, Pages 120-127.

February, 1990 – NAACP – Black Achiever Award

February, 1990 – *Tallahassee Democrat* – "Hand of A Fighter"

January, 1991 – *Tallahassee Democrat* – Tallahasseans Gather to Honor King and Steele

November, 1991 – *Tallahassee Democrat* – "Sister, You've Done a Good Job"

November, 1991 – Board of County Commissioners – Birthday Resolution

November, 1991 – City of Gretna, Key to the City

August, 1992 – Capital Outlook – "Why I Support Dave Lang"

January, 1994 – National Women of Achievement – Outstanding Service Award

March, 1994 – Tallahassee Chapter, National Hookup of Black Women – Gold Star Award

March, 1995 – *Church Times* – Rev Bernyce Clausell, History of Calvary Church

April, 1995 – *Capital Outlook* –"Clausell, Stephens receive Living Legend Award"

April, 1996 – 19th Annual Bond Day By Day Program – Recognition by Barbara Bozeman

September, 1996 – Tallahassee Area Church News – Personal Interview on Clausell Retirement

October, 1996 – Innovation Church Prison Ministry –Certificate of Appreciation

November, 1996 – *Tallahassee Democrat* – "I Heard God Speak"

November, 1996 – Church Times – An Excerpted Autobiography of Rev. Bernyce Clausell

November, 1996 – *Tallahassee Democrat* "Overcoming the Odds"

December, 1996 – Capital Outlook – "Clausell Honored with Celebration"

December, 1996 – *Capital Outlook* – "Tallahassee's Mother Teresa Says Farewell to Friends"

Jan 1997 – *Capital Outlook* – "Clausell to Receive M.L. King Award"

January, 1997 – *Tallahassee Democrat* – Rev. Clausell given M.L. King Award

February 1997 – Recipient of Governor Lawton Chiles' Florida's Finest Award

November, 1997 – *Tallahassee Democrat* – FAMU Salutes It's Living Legends for Homecoming '97

February, 1998 – *Tallahassee Democrat* – "Preacher who helped the needy loses her home in fire"

February, 1998 – *Capital Outlook* – "Fire Strikes"

February, 1998 – *Tallahassee Democrat* – Reverend gets outpouring of Support

February, 1998 – *Tallahassee Democrat* – Community rallies for the Rev. Clausell

April, 1998 – Florida State Hospital – Volunteer Service Award

April, 1998 – *Capital Outlook* – Women of rare courage and strength

August, 1998 – Tallahassee Frontiers – Distinguished Service Award

October, 1998 – Bond Day By Day Appreciation Award

March, 2001 – Tallahassee Drifters – Star of the Universe Award

February, 2002 – *Tallahassee Democrat* – "TCC honors black achievers with calendar

June, 2002 – National Association of University Women – Community Service Award

December, 2002 – *Church Times* – Rev. Bernyce Clausell, The Black Mother Teresa

January, 2003 – Southern Christian Leadership Conference – Lifetime Achievement Award

April, 2003 – 25th Anniversary Volunteer of the year finalist

May, 2003 – Great Recoveries, Barbara Bozeman Director, Community Award

December, 2003 – Greater Mt. Pleasant Heart to Heaven Outreach Ministry-Dedicated Service

February, 2004 – Ministers and Laypersons Union – African American Trailblazer Award

March, 2004 – Tallahassee Kwanzaa Association Celebration of Afro American Women Award

May, 2004 – *Tallahassee Democrat* – Honoring History, Freedom

June, 2004 – *Capital Outlook* – Church co-founder honored at Appreciation service.

July, 2004 – *Tallahassee Democrat* – Women of the Word

August, 2004 – Tallahassee Democrat - Mother-Daughter Team will lead Revival

October, 2004 – Ministers & Laypersons Union – Recognition of Appreciation & Support

November, 2004 – Bill Montford & School District of Leon County – Proclamation

February, 2005 – Doris Hobbs -Tabernacle COCWIH, Gretna, Florida – Black History Award

April, 2005 –Tribute by Rev. Arthur Stephens for Outstanding Community Service

May, 2005 – Pastor Barbara Awoniyi New Life UMC – Dynamic Woman Plaque

June, 2005 – National Association of University Women – Devoted Member Award

February 2006 – *Tallahassee Democrat* – Black History Month feature article

May, 2006 – 100 Black Men – Living Legend Award

May, 2006 – Mary Brogan Museum Exhibit – Wisdom of the Ages

August, 2006 – *Tallahassee Democrat* – "Church set to clear out give-away program"

November, 2006 – City of Tallahassee – Proclamation – Bernyce H. Clausell Day

November, 2006 – *Tallahassee Democrat* – "Celebrating A Life - Turning 90"

November, 2006 – *Gadsden County Times* -"She Made A Difference In Gretna"

November, 2006 – Bishop Alvin Stewart-Abundant Life Ministries – Birthday Recognition

November, 2006 – Kings Cross Victory Bible College – Honorary Doctor of Divinity

December, 2006 – Board of Leon County Commissioners – Resolution of Congratulations

December, 2006 – Church Women United – Human Rights Award

February, 2007 – Innovation School of Excellence – Legacy and Achievement Award

March, 2007 – National Association of University Women – Founders Day Award

March, 2008 – *Tallahassee Democrat* – "On Church's 50th Anniversary, Clausell realizes a dream"

March, 2008 – Calvary Baptist Church – 50th Anniversary -The Dreamer Plaque

May 2008 – *Tallahassee Democrat* – "It's Always Good To Celebrate Freedom"

September, 2008 – *Tallahassee Democrat* – Local Pastors

November, 2008 – Picture featured on United States Postage Stamp

February, 2009 – Capital Outlook – "Big Spirit"

March, 2009 – Rev. DeWayne Harvey & Greater Blessings Church-Women of Light Award

March,2009 – *Tallahassee Democrat* – The Oasis Center honors Trailblazing Women

April, 2009 – Pastor Rosalyn Thompkins & President Obama's National Service Council, presented the Presidential Volunteer Service Award to Rev. Clausell

June 2009 – Women of Promise presented Certificate of Recognition and Appreciation

September, 2009 – African American Pulpit -Article by Rev. Mallory White - "A Nonagenerian's Journey: An Interview with Rev. Bernyce Clausell

December, 2009 – Clergywomen United – 25+ years Retirement Plaque

February, 2010 – The Peterson Family presented "Living Legend Award"

June, 2010 – Tallahassee Girl's Choir of Choice - "Silver Sisters Role Model Award"

October, 2010- NAACP Freedom Banquet – Honored among Five "Mothers of the Movement"

November, 2010 – Mayor John Marks presented Mayor's Meritorius Achievement Award

November, 2010 – *Tallahassee Democrat* – "Clausell Celebrates 94 years with sermon and new ministry"

March, 2011 – Jefferson County Correction Institution – Certificate of Recognition

March, 2011 – Gospel Truth Magazine – Article by Shannon Ferrell,"Rev. Clausell, A Remarkable Woman of God"